KU-444-423

GALORE PARK

Step by Step
Reading

by Mona McNee

www.galorepark.co.uk

Published by Galore Park Publishing Ltd
19/21 Sayers Lane, Tenterden, Kent TN30 6BW

www.galorepark.co.uk
Text copyright © Galore Park 2006
Illustrations copyright Galore Park 2006

The right of Mona McNee to be identified as the author of this Work has been asserted by her in accordance with sections 77 and 78 of the Copyright, Designs and Patents Act 1988.

Design and typesetting by Design Gallery, Suffolk
Illustrations by Rosie Brooks and Gwyneth Williamson

Printed by CPI, Glasgow

ISBN-13: 978 1 902984 83 4

All rights reserved: no part of this publication may be reproduced, stored in a retrieval system, or transmitted in any form or by any means, electronic, mechanical, photocopying, recording or otherwise, without either the prior written permission of the copyright owner or a licence permitting restricted copying issued by the Copyright Licencing Agency, 90 Tottenham Court Road, London W1P 0LP.

This edition published 2007

Available from Galore Park:
English
French
History
Latin
Maths
Science
Spanish

Preface

My son Tim has Down's syndrome. He was my first pupil and he taught me how to teach reading. I was told his IQ was 65, and he didn't learn to read at school. So I started teaching him myself, untrained, using simple phonics. His progress never halted. After 18 months he could read – and I had to tell the school! They tested him, and found he really could read.

He has borrowed books from the library all his life. He borrows and buys books on history, he reads what he wants to in the newspaper, finds TV programmes, reads maps and road signs, like we all do. His life now would be very different if he could not read. Intensive, systematic phonics saved him from a life of illiteracy. This book will show you how.

You will find that throughout the book, the pupil is referred to as 'he'. This, of course, is not to suggest that your pupil cannot be female, but is to avoid the distracting use of 'he/she'.

Mona McNee

Contents

Introduction

Steps

Learning to read with phonics

This book uses synthetic phonics to teach reading. It will enable you to teach your child, an adult or even a class of children or adults to read. You do not need training, just common sense and the will to teach (not to help, encourage or facilitate, but specifically to teach) reading using phonics.

Teaching children, or adults, to read is simple and does not take long. You just need a structured phonics programme. You start at the beginning, with letters and sounds. The pupil learns how to sound out, how to blend three sounds in a word, how to make 'c - a - t' into 'cat', then longer words. This is the most important part. Your pupil will learn letters one at a time, and at the same time will write them, sound them out and learn to blend the sounds into words, and to break words down into sounds which he can then spell.

Once your pupil can read words like 'comic' and 'hundred', he will have completed the first third of learning to read. He will know that *he* can get the word from the letters, not from the picture, and that *he* can do it; he does not need someone else to tell him what the words are. Both teacher and pupil will know exactly where they are up to, and what the next task is. There is fun in the games described in this book, but the main incentive is success. It is exciting.

The second part of learning to read is to learn those sounds for which we use two or more letters, 'sh' as in 'fish', 'aw' as in 'crawl', and so on. When your pupil can hear the sounds in words, he will know the letters that represent them and will therefore be able to spell correctly the 90 per cent of words that conform to the basic rules of phonics.

The final third is gaining fluency, and it is at this point that great benefit arises from reading, and practice. By this time, an element of self-tutoring has developed and usually there is no looking back. It is rather like pushing a bicycle up a hill: when you get to the top, you can enjoy free-wheeling down a lovely, long slope. It gets easier.

When to start

Starting this *simple* way, with letters and sounds, children are ready to learn to read by their fourth birthday if not before. All children should learn to read, write and spell regular and common words in two years or less. So, ready at their fourth birthday, children should be reading by their sixth birthday. For children older than six, parents should not accept the advice, 'Don't worry. He'll catch on. It's early days yet.' It is the early learning that gives the automaticity we need when we want to read to learn. And worldwide, millions have failed to learn to read, for lack of early, systematic, synthetic, simple phonics. The sooner children start, the better.

If your child can match up the letters (see Using the alphabet card and letter cards, page viii), and he is talking, he is ready to start learning to read. If he is three and not talking, teaching him to read by this method is a form of speech therapy and can help him to learn to talk at the same time. Using this book can also correct speech in order to improve spelling (saying 'think' instead of 'fink', for instance).

How long will it take?

It will of course take some people longer than it will take others. Older children, for example, will not need to spend much time on the letters. Just make sure that they do know 26 letters, and the 'kw' sounds for 'qu', that they get 'b/d' right, 'p/q', and 'y'.

It may sound silly to say that if someone learns quickly, he will learn more quickly, but if too much time elapses (three or four days) between one lesson and the next, the learning fades. Also, if someone learns quickly, he is aware of his progress and that is an incentive. If the learning is slow, the pupil is not aware of progress and feels he is just plodding on without getting anywhere. An hour a day for ten days gives more progress than the same ten hours spread over 20 days. You may wish to make a note in this book of the date on which you do each step. Your pupil will then be able to see how quickly he has progressed.

How to use this book

This book is set out as a series of 50 steps. Some steps will take just one lesson; others will take longer.

Always read through what you intend to cover with your pupil before you start (ideally the day before) to make sure you are prepared. As well as the alphabet card and letter cards which I use throughout the course, there are a large number of resources and games which can help to make learning fun. Visit our website www.galorepark.co.uk for details. Feel free to use your own ideas too, and remember that throughout, both you and your pupil should be enjoying yourselves. Pour out the praise endlessly.

The first 14 steps take you through the 26 letters of the alphabet: how to write each one, and its sound. I recommend teaching at least one letter a day, perhaps up to four letters a day. I do not teach 'a' then 'b' then 'c, d, e' because this makes 'b' and 'd' very close together (they are often confused). I begin the steps with 'c' and four letters that start with the same action as 'c' ('a, d, g' and 'o'). The letter 'b' is left nearly to the end with the letters 'h' and 'k'. I leave 'q' until last because there is no simple three-letter word with a 'q' in it. Steps 15 to 50 introduce other sounds and rules that will enable your pupil to read and spell most words.

If your pupil gets stuck or makes a mistake, avoid saying 'No' or 'That's wrong'. See if any of it is right. Comment on all the things that are right; do not praise without justification, but find *something* to praise. If it is 'just one of those days', laugh and say, 'Well, tomorrow is another day.'

Aim for at least 30 minutes a day, but don't feel you must stick rigidly to this. Use your judgment. On good days you may do an hour, on other days just ten minutes, but try to do a bit each day, even if it is only a game. Varied activity extends the span of attention and therefore the lesson.

Using the alphabet card and letter cards

Towards the back of this book you will find an alphabet card and some letters. You will use these throughout the book. Set out the letters on the alphabet card, pick out each letter as it is learned and then show where it goes on the alphabet. Using the alphabet card also helps to teach the positions of the letters in the alphabet; you will be surprised how quickly your pupil learns the position for each letter.

At first, you will give your pupil just one letter to match up by its shape. When he can do this easily, give him a handful of letters and get him to match them up on the alphabet card. Seeing the 26 letters shows that learning the letters is finite; he can see how many he has to learn. This feels much more achievable than learning whole words. One boy who was learning in this way asked his mother how many words there were, and she replied, 'Oh, I don't know – thousands!' He gave up.

Using the letters is a painless way to improve spelling. The pupil can pick out letters for sounds he can hear, and instead of red ink on mistakes, you just have to rearrange letters, or let him rearrange them, or take out wrong letters, and leave a space for a missing letter. He then has to listen to the word and *hear* how the spoken word does not match the letters he has chosen, and to *hear* what letters he needs to provide the missing sounds.

Pronunciation

When learning to read, your pupil will need to use the sound of the letters rather than their names – 'a' as in 'cat' rather than 'a' as in 'say'. You can refer to the names of the letters too, but it is the sounds that are blended together to make words. Once your pupil has learned how to pronounce each sound, you teach him to blend the sounds into words. You also teach them how to break words down into sounds, which they can then spell.

Writing

Each letter that you teach in this book is accompanied by a dot-to-dot illustration of how the letter should be written. On the dot-to-dot letter, show how you start drawing at the arrow and move in the direction that the arrow points. The dots show where there should be a flowing line, not a jerky dot-to-dot join. Where there are dashes, you go there and back, in two directions. If there is only one arrow, the whole letter is completed before lifting the pencil from the page, as in 'c' and 'a'.

Show how letters are made up of straight lines and parts of a circle:

Straight lines: 'l', 'x', 'v', 'w', 'z'.
Circle (or part of): 'o', 'c', 's'.
and combinations of both.

Show that the letters 'sit on a line', and that you begin on the left side. If a young child has not yet learned left and right, put a marker of some kind (a paper clip) on the left side of the paper, and say, 'You start at this side.' If this left-right direction is pointed out at the start, and a finger points out the letters or words as you work, there is usually not a problem. Prevention of confusion with 'saw/was', 'of/for/from' depends on what you do at the beginning: the left-right direction must become automatic. Once your pupil has practised writing the letter using the dot-to-dot guide, he should practise writing the letter on guidelines. A workbook with guidelines is ideal for this or you can print off extra guidelines from the website if they are needed.

How to hold a pencil

Before your pupil starts to write, make sure that he has the correct pencil grip the *first* time he holds a crayon or pencil. The thumb and side of the long (middle) finger do the gripping, with the index finger sitting loosely on top. Prevent bad habits. If pencil grip is a problem, try a triangular pencil-grip. Left-handed writers will probably need to have their paper more slanted (left side higher) than for right-handed people.

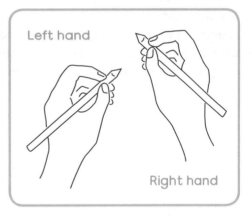

Left hand

Right hand

Teach your pupil to write each letter by going over the dot-to-dot letters with a pencil. He can also trace over the shape with his finger, so that his muscles become familiar with the movements required.

If your pupil is pressing too hard on the paper, turn the page over and let him feel the ridges he has made. Tell him pressing hard will make him tired. Buy a propelling pencil with a thin lead, so that it breaks when he presses too hard. This works when nagging does not.

Try these

Every time you teach another letter or group of letters, you are widening the vocabulary that your pupil can read. The 'Try these' sections list some of these new words and suggests that your pupil makes these new words using the letter cards. The letters should be replaced on the alphabet card in the correct position after each new word has been made.

As your pupil reads through the lists of words, he must say each word, pronounce it correctly, and either know what it means or ask you if he is not sure. Many children think that saying the word is enough, and do not ask for the meaning. Asking must be strongly encouraged. Emphasise that asking for the meaning is a sign of intelligence and common sense, not a sign of being stupid.

Exercises

These give your pupil the opportunity to practise what you have taught. Sometimes he has to fill in letters in a word, sometimes match words to pictures. The instructions are for your pupil to read, though you may have to read them to him at first.

A final word

Teaching someone to read is one of the greatest gifts you can give. By following this course you will be opening up a whole world of opportunities to your pupil. Even when it seems hard work, always remember how grateful he will be. And remember, enjoy it all the way through, step by step.

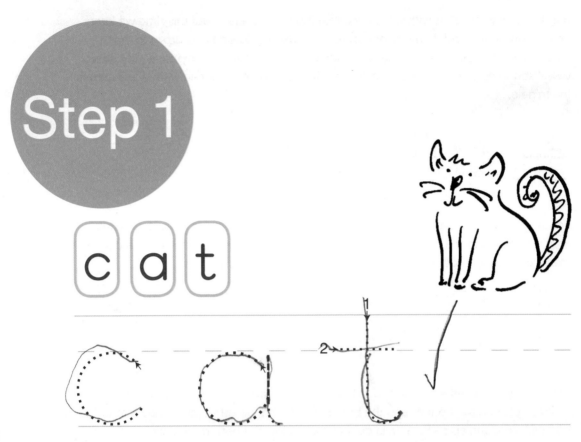

Step 1

c a t

Show your pupil the dot-to-dot letters 'c a t' above. (See page ix for instructions on how to follow the dot-to-dot guides.) Explain to the pupil that you can have a real, live cat, you have the spoken word 'cat' and thanks to a wonderful invention called letters, you can also write the word 'cat'. There are 26 letters to learn, and in this step we will learn three of them: 'c', 'a', and 't'.

c Get your pupil to draw a 'c' in the air, swinging his arms from the shoulder, and say 'kuh'. Ideally we would try to sound the 'k' sound without the 'uh', but it is not easy, and the extra sound does not bother most people. If you wish him to learn 'c' says 'kuh', the name and the sound, you can. In the end he will have to know both name and sound, but at the beginning it is the sounds that are essential.

Show on a round clock how 'c' starts not at the top, not at 12 o'clock, but at 2 o'clock, and goes back up and round to 6 and up to 4. The capital is the same, only bigger.

a For the 'a' say 'We start with a 'c', the same movement again, but this time we keep going, right round and then straight up to the broken guideline and down to the bottom line, and this is an 'a'. Get your pupil to draw it in the air saying 'a', the short vowel sound as in 'cat'. The capital letter is like a pointed mountain, with a line across the middle.

t For the 't' point out that there are two beginnings: first a downward one, then a left-right one. Show that the cross on the 't' goes along the broken guideline. The capital starts with the left-right move at the top and then comes down.

Point out how the letters sit on the bottom line. The circle part of the letters fits exactly between the bottom and the broken lines. The tall letters reach down from the top guideline, and some have tails going down below the bottom guideline.

Let your pupil go over each letter many times, with his finger, with a pale coloured crayon or felt pen and then with a darker pen. Let him practise on the guidelines or in a workbook. He must go over a letter, look at it, sound it, hear it, all at the same time.

At the same time your pupil becomes familiar with the three sounds from writing them and sounding them out, you must introduce the idea that 'c-a-t' makes cat. He must be able to hear the bits and join them, and hear that 'cat' starts with the 'c' sound, then 'a', then 't'.

Try these

cat   at   act

Set out the alphabet card, pick out the three small letter cards to make the word 'cat' and then show how you put the letters back in their place. Then do the same for the other words above.

Step 2

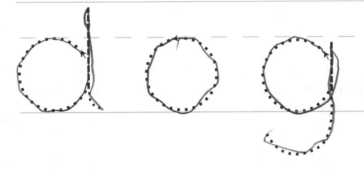

d Write the three new letters large in the air while saying the sounds. Get your pupil to sound out 'd', 'o' and 'g'. Show your pupil how 'd' goes up tall and then comes down again; 'd' is the only letter that goes up tall; all the other tall letters come down. For the capital, come down first, and then make the semi-circle, clockwise from the top.

o Show your pupil how 'o' sits neatly between the lines. Start the 'o' at twelve o'clock and go round anti-clockwise. The capital is the same, but bigger.

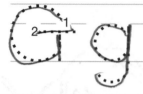 Show your pupil how 'g' starts like an 'o', and then goes up before dropping its tail down below the line. The capital begins with the anti-clockwise semi-circle and downward movement, before the crossbar is added.

Try these
Set out the alphabet card and pick out the six small letter cards that you have covered so far. Put them in the correct places on the alphabet. Ask your pupil to pick out the letters to make the following words:

a	cat	cog	got	cod
at	cot	dog	god	tot
act	tag	dot	to	

He will be learning how letters work, the left to right direction and where the letters belong in the alphabet. Point out that, knowing only six letters, he can already read more than ten words. Teach your pupil to sound the sounds of the new words.

Irregular words
Note that 'to' is an irregular word. Your pupil can see the 't' and hear it work, but explain that 'It looks like 'to' (the beginning of 'top') but we say 'too'.

Get your pupil to write the words below.

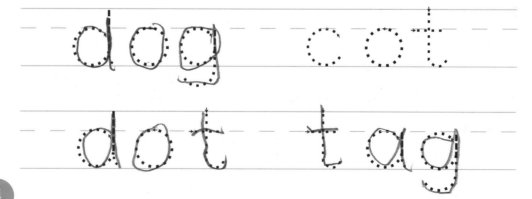

Step 3

f x

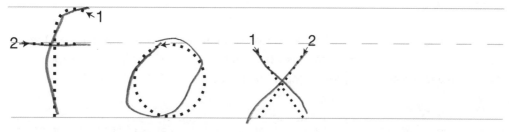

f Explain that 'f' begins above the broken line with the top of a circle, and we go 'back up, over, round and down', (not down and up like an 'r'). The capital starts with the downward movement, followed by lines to the right at the top and middle.

X Show your pupil to start the 'x' at the top of the left-hand line, lift off, and then go to the top of the right-hand line. Sometimes children find it hard to make the parts of an 'x' slope down properly. Practising with a box will help this. Show how 'x' fits into a box. The capital is the same, only bigger.

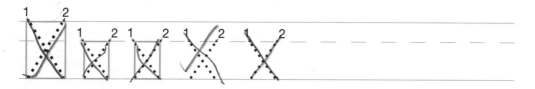

Try these

Add the two new letters to the alphabet card and let your pupil make the following new words:

fat   fad   fog   cox   box

If your pupil forgets a letter, go back to where he learned it, let him sound out the letter and remind himself what it says. Note that, if you teach 'a' for 'apple' or 'Annie Apple', your pupil can end up thinking 'a' says 'apple' (or 'Annie'), giving too much importance to the first letter. This is why I use a few words in which the pupil can learn the letters, with all the letters equally important. In this way the left-right direction is reinforced and your pupil is hearing sounds in words all the time.

Note also that clear speech helps spelling. For example, 'f' is said by biting the bottom lip. This must be clearly fixed to the letter 'f', so that when 'th' is introduced, it sounds quite different.

Note that 'x' is the only letter that makes two sounds: 'ks' or when voiced, 'gz'. Let the pupil hear the 'x' sound in other words such as 'fix', 'mix', 'six', 'next', 'exact', 'exit', 'expand', 'expect'. Explain these if necessary.

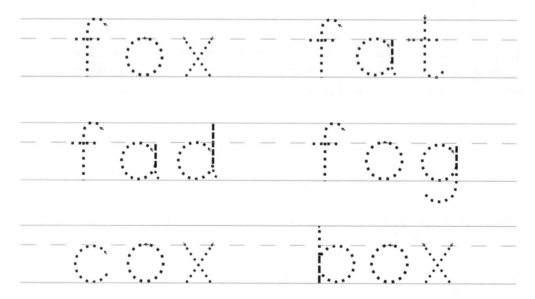

Step 4

v n

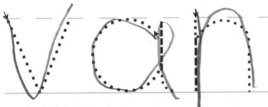

v
Show this picture of a valley, explain what a valley is and then show that a 'v' is the shape of a valley. Talk through going up a mountain and down the other side: the point is at the top. Then talk through moving between two mountains, going down into the valley, and up the next mountain. A valley is the opposite of a mountain, and has the point at the bottom. Emphasise that the point should not be a curve. The 'v' is made of two straight lines, down and then up. The capital is the same, only bigger.

1
Vv

n
Draw the 'n' starting at the top left, go down, back up again and over the top in a nice curve and down the other side. Show your pupil how it looks like an arch. The capital is three straight lines. The ones on the outside should be vertical.

12
Nn

Try these

Show how knowing two more letters gives access to many more words. Add the two new letters to the alphabet card. Revise the sounds of all the letters learned so far and then let your pupil make the following new words:

can   nag   not

fan   tan   and

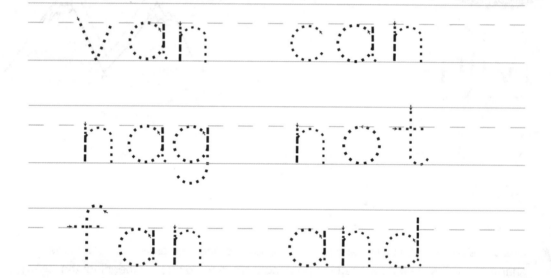

Now try these

Your pupil can already start to read short phrases:

A tag on a dog   A dog and a cot

A cot and a van   A dog on a van

Step 5

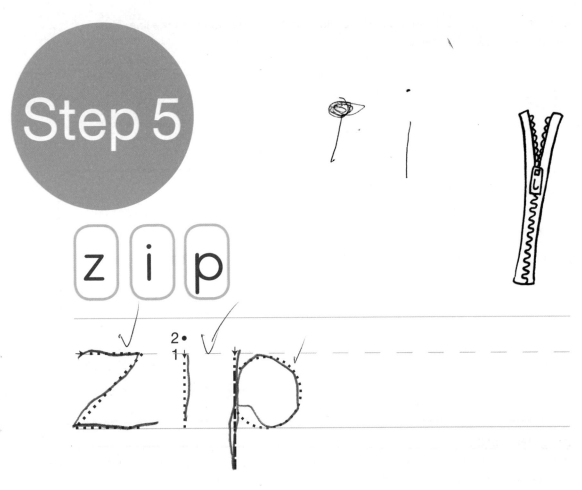

z i p

z Sometimes children find it hard to make the parts of a 'z' slope down properly. Practising with a box will help this. Show how 'z' fits into a square box. The capital is the same, only bigger.

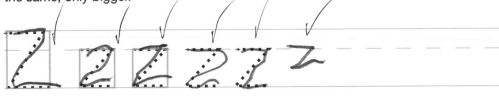

i Draw the 'i' with the downstroke first and then the dot. It should be a dot, not a circle. The capital is just one long downstroke.

p

Draw the 'p' by going down, up and around, with the circle sitting on the line. The capital is very similar, only bigger.

Try these

Add the three new letters to the alphabet card, and let your pupil make the following new words:

tip	dig	fig	pig	cap
pod	pat	pot	top	fit
pit	fizz			

Point out that if there are two of the same consonants next to one another, you only sound them out once.

Irregular words

Point out that the letter 'i' when used on its own is always written as a capital letter. When it is read out the sound it makes is the name of the letter.

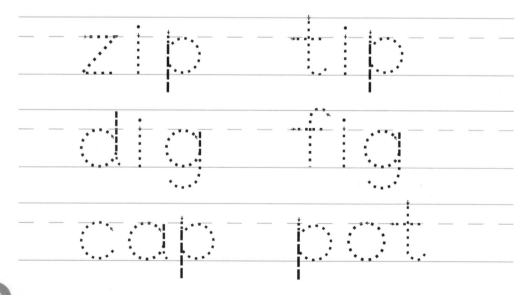

Step 6

w e

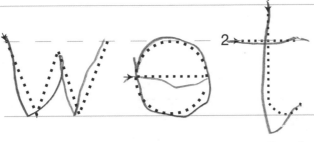

W Point out that a 'w' is rather like two 'v's – the French even call it 'double v'! Point out that when the letter 'w' is printed the points are sharp at the bottom, but when it is written in handwriting they are curved (which is why we call it a 'double u'). The capital always has sharp points.

e With 'e', make sure your pupil starts in the middle of the letter and finishes at the bottom. Point out that once he has made the first left to right stroke, the rest of the letter is just like a 'c'. The capital begins with the downstroke, and then across the bottom followed by two lines going to the right at the top and middle.

Try these
Add the two new letters to the alphabet card. Let your pupil make the following new words:

net   vet   get
pet   den   ten

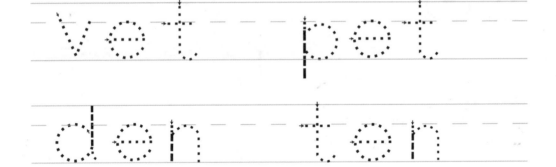

How are we doing?
Point out to your pupil that he now knows 15 letters, and is over half-way through the alphabet. The letters he knows are shown below in blue.

a	b	c	d	e	f	g	h	i	j	k
l	m	n	o	p	q	r	s	t	u	v
w	x	y	z							

Step 7

r

The letter 'r' starts at the top, and goes down, up and over. It does not start on the line at the bottom. It has the same movement as an 'n' but stops short. The capital starts in the same way, going down, up and over, then continues round to meet the downards line halfway. A third line then drops down as shown below.

Try these
Add the new letter to the alphabet card and let your pupil make the following new words:

rip   rod   rid   ran   rot

Step 8

m

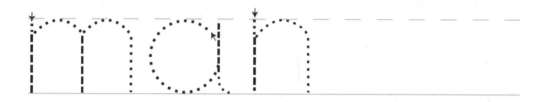

m Sound 'm' with the lips closed, humming, not 'mer' ('mer' has two sounds 'm'-'er'). The capital is like the smal 'm' made up of four straight lines. The first line down, then lifting the pen off and restarting at the same point and then going down, up, down.

Show how 'm', 'n' and 'r' all start the same, by moving down and then up.

Try these
Add the new letter to the alphabet card and let your pupil make the following new words:

mat	ram	dam
dim	mop	map

Step 9

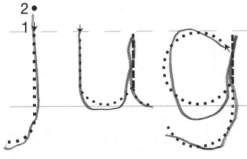

j Show how to draw 'j', adding the dot on top. The capital is similar, but instead of a dot we add a crossbar. Sound the sound, not the name.

u When sounding the letter 'u', be sure to make the sound (with a short sound as in 'gun'), not the name. Say "u' goes under and up'. Show how to draw the 'u' as one movement, down, up and down again. The capital is one simple movement, down and up.

Try these
Add the two new letters to the alphabet card and let your pupil make the following new words:

rug	mug	cup	but	puff
dug	up	pup	jet	jot
jam				

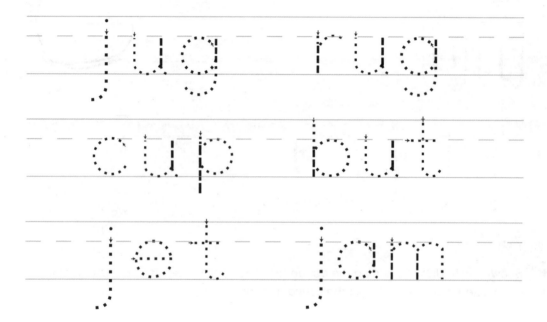

Step 10

l

Teach that the letter 'l' is a long line. Let the pupil reach high into the air and then come down to draw an 'l'. You may wish to point out that it looks just like a capital 'i'. The capital 'L' is the same but with a line at the bottom to the right. Point out that many words have double 'l', such as 'pull', 'doll', 'pill' etc. When you have two letters together like this making the same sound, you only say the sound once.

Try these
Add the new letter to the alphabet card and let your pupil make the following new words:

let	lit	lot	lap	log
leg	lag	lad	pull	doll

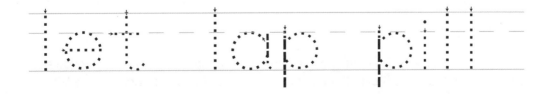

Step 11

h k b

h Point out that these three letters all start with the shape of an 'l'. Tell your pupil that 'h' is the blowy letter. Show how it starts by coming down like 'l' and then goes up and over the arch like 'n'. For the capital, do the two downward lines and then join them in the middle with the crossbar.

k Point out that a 'k' has two (not three) starts: down and off, then in, out and off. The capital is the same, only bigger.

Explain that when a 'k' is at the end of a short, one-syllable word with a short vowel, we must put a 'c' in front of it. Point out that if you have a sound twice ('c' and 'k'), you only say it once.

b

Teach 'b' by showing this picture of a bat and a ball.

For older children (and adults who have confused 'b' and 'd'), show that they are not the same. Only one starts at the top, a 'b'. You draw a straight line down (a bat) and on the right of it you draw the ball, so that the bat can hit the ball along the empty line or along the line the way we read. The pupil must think 'bat and a ball - 'b".

The letter 'd' is different. It starts with a 'c' and it is the only letter where we draw up to the tall part, and do not start with a down movement. If your pupil knows the order of the letters at the beginning of the alphabet: 'a, b, c, d', show him how to tap out the 'a', 'b' with his non-writing hand, and then draw the 'c' and keep going to make a 'd'. To get a 'd' right, he must say to himself 'a, b, c, d'. See Step 2.

Exercise 11.1
Practise writing these words:

pack	peck	pick	lock	duck
rack	deck	tick	rock	buck
back	neck	lick	mock	puck
hack		kick	dock	luck
tack		nick		suck

Exercise 11.2

Sort out the letters to make a word.

 guj ___ ___ ___

 nva ___ ___ ___

 tco ___ ___ ___

 act ___ ___ ___

 ent ___ ___ ___

 pzi ___ ___ ___

Step 12

s

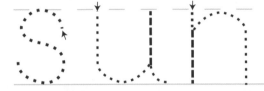

S Show that an 's' fits inside a circle. The top bend of the 's' should be, if anything, smaller and tighter, than the bottom bend. Point out that 's' is the shape of a snake, and it makes the same sound. The capital is the same, only bigger.

Try these

Add the new letter to the alphabet card and let your pupil make the following new words:

sat	set	sun	cup	sip
sad	sag	gas	sick	sock
suck	ask			

Plurals

Say the following words in the singular (one) and plural (more than one):

hat   hats

peg   pegs

dog   dogs

Encourage your pupil to hear that by putting an 's' after a word, we make the word plural.

Verbs

Also show how the 's' is used in verbs:

run   runs

hit   hits

dig   digs

Explain that we say:
'I run, you run', but 'he runs'.
'I dig, you dig', but 'he digs'.

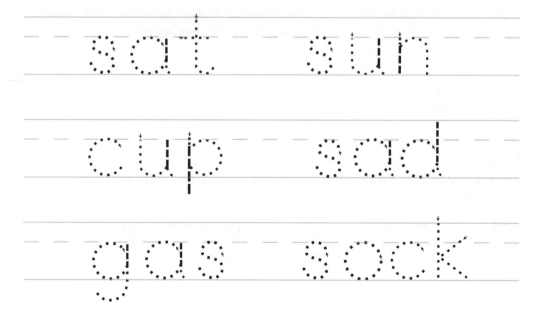

Step 13

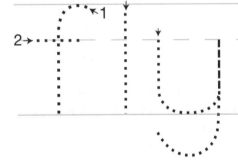

Teach your pupil how a 'y' starts like 'u' and then has a tail that comes down below the line. The capital is formed with two (not three) straight lines.

The letter 'y' can make the sound of a vowel or the sound of a consonant. At the beginning of a word or syllable (as in 'yes', 'yellow', 'beyond', 'crayon') 'y' is a consonant. As a vowel, the letter 'y' makes the same two sounds that 'i' makes: the long sound in 'fly', 'cry' and 'satisfy' and the short sound in 'system' and 'happy'.

Most teachers teach the letter 'y' as a consonant ('y' says 'yer'), but this does not work with the many words ending in 'y' (long 'i' sound), e.g. 'happy', 'funny', 'quickly' or with those containing a 'y' such as 'bicycle' or 'system' (short 'i' sound). So start by teaching the vowel sounds that 'y' makes. When children learn only 'yer' for 'y', they end up sounding 'happy' as 'happ-yer', etc., and do not get the meaning. While few words start with 'y' (consonant), hundreds of words have the vowel 'y' in the middle and end.

Capital letters for names

The easiest words to show as having the vowel sound of 'y' are names, so now is the time to talk about capital letters. All letters have a small (lower case) or capital (upper case) form. Names always begin with a capital, so to write his name your pupil needs to use the capitals.

Try these

Harry	Henry	Polly
Billy	Sandy	Betty
Jenny	Patsy	Barry

You have been meeting all the capital letters, while learning the small ones. Many of these are little more than bigger versions of the small ones, but others, as you will have noticed, are slightly different. Here is a reminder:

a b c d e f g h i j k l m n o p q r s t u v w x y z

A B C D E F G H I J K L M N O P Q R S T U V W X Y Z

There is one letter you have not yet learnt, 'q', we will now do so in the next step.

Step 14

This is the big day, the very last letter, so make a big fuss!

Teach your pupil how the tail of 'q' comes down below the line, and then ends with a little upward stroke. This upward stroke will be needed when doing joined-up writing. The capital is a big circle with a line coming out of it.

In English words, the letter 'q' is always followed by a 'u', and the two letters together usually say 'kw'.

Try these

Add the final letter to the alphabet card, making all 26 letters. Let your pupil make the following new words, reminding the pupil that the 'kw' sound has two letters 'qu'.

quiz   quick   quack   quit

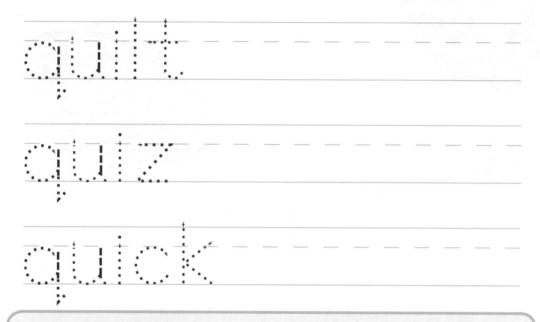

Additional Resources

Your pupil is now ready to use Set 1 of the Step by Step Reading Additional Resources. See the website or the accompanying instructions for details of how to use these.

Sing along

Now that your pupil knows all the letters, sing the alphabet song over and over until he really knows the order of the letters. The tune below ('Mary, Mary, quite contrary') is the best one to use to keep each letter nice and distinct. As you sing the song, touch each letter as you sing it, and practise with the capital letters too.

Vowel table

You can now tell your pupil that five of the letters he has learnt, 'a', 'e', 'i', 'o' and 'u', are called vowels. These vowels give the sounds 'ay', 'ee', 'i', 'oh' and 'you'. All the rest are consonants. 'Y' is sometimes a vowel (as in 'fly'), sometimes a consonant (as in 'yes'). Use this vowel table to help your pupil with both reading and spelling. I tell pupils that they read with their ears, and even more, they spell with their ears. Say a simple three-letter word (e.g. 'dot', 'jug', 'lip', 'mug', 'tap', 'gun', 'zip', 'van', 'fan', 'hat', 'six') to your pupil and ask him to listen for the vowel in the middle. He should then find the correct column and try to write in the word. You can use any words that have three letters. Avoid words like 'fur' that have three letters but only two sounds, or 'was' where the 'wa' does not make the sound in 'wax'. Where possible, let your pupil do his own checking.

The aim is plenty of practice so that the response to a three-letter word becomes automatic and fast.

a	e	i	o	u

Your pupil is now ready to try the following exercises and practise writing. If the child is pressing too hard when writing, turn the page over and let him feel the ridges he has made. Buy a cheap propelling pencil with a thin lead so that it breaks when he presses too hard. You can also try out simple dictation, single words, phrases or sentences like: 'A dog can run. A pig is fat. Pat has a red hat. Jim got wet.' Make up your own.

Exercise 14.1

Draw a line from each word to the correct picture.

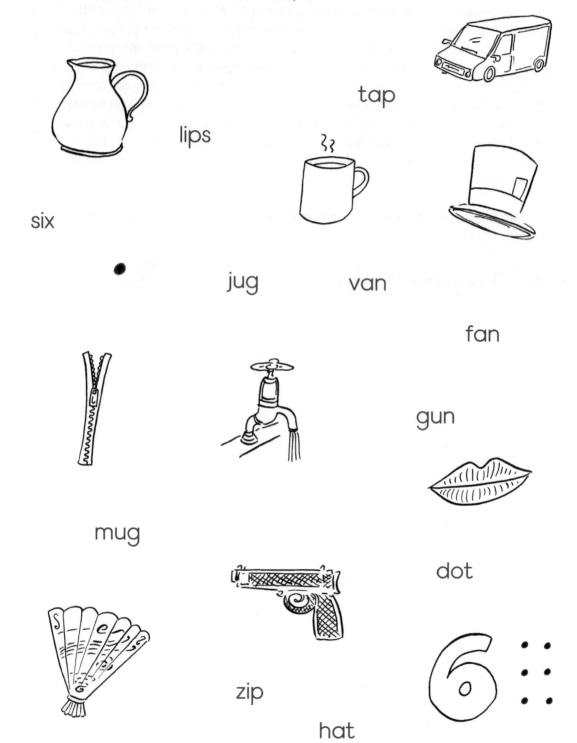

tap

lips

six

jug   van

fan

gun

mug

dot

zip

hat

Exercise 14.2

Add a 'b' or a 't' to each of these words.

b t

_ us

_en

_un

_ox

_op

_ap

Exercise 14.3

Sort out the letters to make a word.

six eggs in a box

o
x
b _ _ _

x
s
i _ _ _

x
f
o _ _ _

Exercise 14.4

Add the correct letters to complete these words.

10 _e_   6 _i_   _u_

_a_   _o_   _a_

Exercise 14.5

Sort out the letters to make a word.

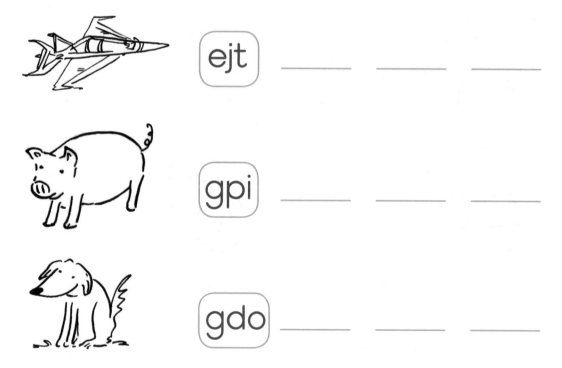

ejt ___ ___ ___

gpi ___ ___ ___

gdo ___ ___ ___

nva _____ _____ _____

nca _____ _____ _____

unr _____ _____ _____

tha _____ _____ _____

umg _____ _____ _____

xsi _____ _____ _____

Exercise 14.6

Say the word for the picture, and listen to the word as you say it. Then spell it from listening to your own voice.

Exercise 14.7

Show two words. Ask which letter has been changed in the second word: the first, the middle or the last? What is the new word?

fox

fix six sit sat pat pan pen peg leg let

net not hot hut put pot rot lot

wet vet set met men man pan ran

run

sun

cut but bat ban bun gun

cat

rat hat ham hum him his hit bit

Step 15

Four-letter words

When your pupil can read and spell three-letter words, begin to work with four-letter words, but again only words that have four sounds, e.g. not 'ship' where the 'sh' is one sound and not 'rake' where the 'e' is silent. If you are using other workbooks alongside this book, avoid exercises that use words involving letter-groups that you have not yet taught. For example, 'fork' cannot be used until you have taught 'or'.

Some reading schemes spend time working on 'consonant blends': 'st', 'sp', 'tr', or 'letter strings': 'str', 'spl'. I believe that if someone really grasps how to read three- and four-letter words, and knows 's' and 't', we do not need to spend extra time learning 'st', which is just two ordinary letters one after the other. Why make it seem difficult? Why provide something extra to learn when we do not need it?

When we come, soon, to what I call letter-groups, where two letters must be read together to make one sound, like 'sh', then is the time to have the pupil notice two letters together, but when reading 'vest', 'flat', 'flag', it is enough to go through the sequence of letters, sound them out and *listen*.

Try these

camp	fast	flag	hand
rang	sack	sand	rest
send	sent	vest	went
drip	fist	lick	limp
list	wink	pink	ring
spin	wind	wing	cost
drop	lock	song	stop
lump	must	jump	just

You could also use these words with the vowel table (see page 27). Read out one at a time, and ask your pupil to listen for the vowel. He should then try to write the word into the correct column.

Exercise 15.1

You are given the first letter of the word. Fill in the rest of the letters to match the pictures.

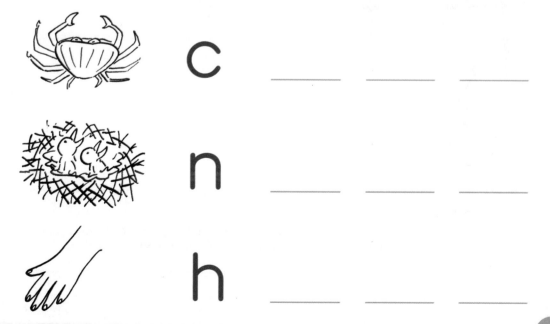

c __ __ __

n __ __ __

h __ __ __

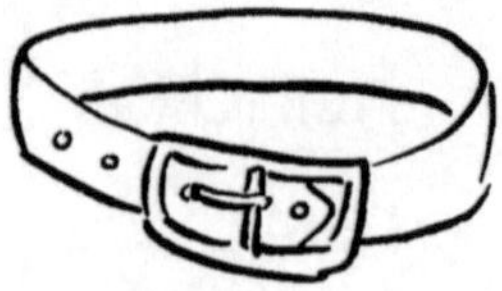

b _____ _____ _____

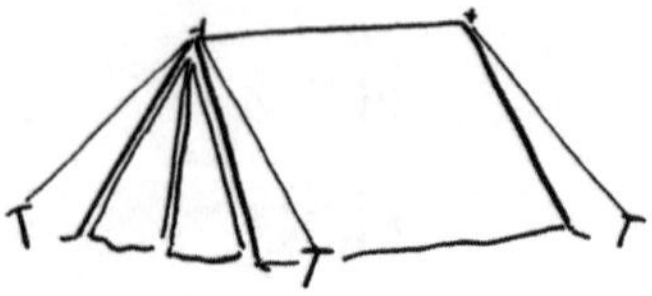

t _____ _____ _____

v _____ _____ _____

f _____ _____ _____

f _____ _____ _____

d _____ _____ _____

Additional resources
Your pupil is now ready to use Set 2 of the Step by Step Reading Additional Resources.
See the website or the accompanying instructions for details of how to use these.

Step 16

Longer words

Your pupil should now be confidently reading words of up to four letters where each letter is making a distinct sound. You now move on to words of five letters: 'stamp', 'crust', 'comic', and then on to words of any length: 'clinic', 'hospital', 'caravan', 'interesting'. At this point you will start to meet words of more than one syllable. Explain to your pupil that a syllable is a word or part of a word that has one vowel sound. You could try to count the syllables in words.

Use your atlas to find longer words that are simply spelled: 'Scotland', 'Finland', 'India', 'Iran', 'Mexico', 'Italy', 'Brazil', 'Florida', 'Mississippi', 'Texas', 'Indiana', 'Atlantic'.

In some words we do not hear a clear vowel sound. We say, for example, 'baskit' and 'sev'n'. It is a good idea to say the word as it is spelt: 'basket', 'seven', making the 'e' say the sound in 'ten', for the first two or three times we say the word. Say:

hos-pi-t<u>a</u>l ('a' as in 'cat')

probl<u>e</u>m ('e' as in 'ten')

Some people need extra practice in listening to, and hearing, sounds in words. Once a week, to increase phonological awareness, practise saying words as follows:

crust	c ... rust
	cr ... ust
	cru ... st
	crus ... t crust

Try these

stamp	stand	swank	basket	trumpet
cramp	nasty	flask	grasp	plant
rabbit	rascal	plank	seven	eleven
expand	empty	lemon	sting	bring
index	swing	drink	comic	problem
along	Frank	bullet	rusty	hundred
crust	stump			

Remind your pupil that if a sound (letter) appears twice, for example a double consonant or a 'ck', you only say the sound once.

Try these

How many of these girls' names do you know?

Anna	Betty	Molly	Linda
Peggy	Polly	Amanda	Brenda
Camilla	Glenda	Matilda	Emma
Olga	Pamela	Edna	Elsa
Veronica	Joanna	Lydia	Stella
Vanessa	Hilda	Sally	Pat
Rebecca	Winifred	Sylvia	Dolly
Hannah	Jessica	Mildred	Kim

Try these

How many of these boys' names do you know?

Alan	Bill	Alec	Brendan	Eric
Harry	Henry	Frank	Fred	Adam
Kit	Ronald	Rex	Sam	Robin
Tom	Colin	Derek	Duncan	Kim
Kevin	Tim	Jim	Max	William
Winston	Trevor	Angus	Ross	Cliff
Jack	Patrick			

Reading or dictation

See if your pupil can read the following. Then dictate it to him and see if he can write it down.

Sam and his family sat on sand. Frank and Sam can swim. A red crab bit Sam. Frank ran to Mum. Dad swam back to help Sam, but a crab still held on! Dad hit a crab and it let go. Sam put a crab back. It ran fast.

Bedtime stories

You can always read stories to children for their pleasure. Now you can start letting your pupil read and puzzle out the words you know he can read (those with no letter-groups). It gets really exciting when he says, 'No, let me do it by myself!' As he learns more letter-groups, he will read more of the words, until he can take over.

But if he starts guessing by using the pictures rather than looking at the letters on the page, try to discourage this as I believe it is a real barrier to progress.

If you are starting to look at books with your pupil, this may be a good time to point out that 'a' is often printed as 'a' and the 'g' is often printed as 'g'. Start by reading some of these short passages to your pupil, and see how much he can read for himself.

A frog is in a pond.
A duck is on a pond.
A rabbit is not in a pond.
A frog can swim.
A duck can swim.
A frog is happy in a pond and
on land.

It is windy.
Wind lifts an umbrella up
and Pam as well.
Pam's dog, Skip, gets wet.

Exercise 16.1

Read the following story. Then fill in the gaps in the story on the next page.

It is hot.
Pam has a long drink of milk.
Pam's dog, Skip, jumps into a
pond and has a long swim.

Skip wets Pam's dress and flops
on grass to rest.
Pam slips on wet grass.

Exercise 16.2
Read the following story and fill in the gaps.

Pam drinks a glass of m_ _ _ .
Skip flops on wet g_ _ss.
The sun is h_ _ .
Skip sw_ _s in a pon_ .
Pa_ sl_ _s on _ _ass.

Pam has a _ _ _ _ , Skip. Skip
smells a _ _ _ _ _ _ . Skip runs
off into a forest. Skip runs in
grass and mud. Pam is upset
until Skip runs back very
muddy but Pam is happy and
hugs him. Skip has a _ _ _ _
on his neck. He cannot get lost.

Exercise 16.3

Try a crossword. Your teacher will help you to read out the clues. If you can't get one answer, go on to the next. (Teachers may choose to teach the word 'the' now – see Step 20.)

1		2		3		4		5		6		7		8		9
10			11				12				13						

Across

2. I wear a _ _ _ on my head.
4. The first colour of the rainbow.
6. We can write with a - - - and ink.
8. Jerry is the mouse; Tom is the _ _ _
10. 5 + 5 = _ _ _
11. A lady carries things in her hand-_ _ _
12. Water comes out of a _ _ _ _
13. The end of your finger is your finger- _ _ _

Down

1. We hit a ball with a _ _ _
2. The _ _ _ laid an egg.
3. Americans call a bath a _ _ _
4. A _ _ _ is a small carpet.
5. We learn to write using _ _ _ to _ _ _ patterns.
6. A young dog is a _ _ _
7. We can have a Brazil _ _ _ , hazel _ _ _, chest _ _ _ _
8. The captain on a ship wears a _ _ _ _
9. We climbed the hill to the very _ _ _

Exercise 16.4

Write the correct word beside each picture. Remember that if a consonant sound appears twice, you only say it once, e.g. 'pocket', 'bucket', 'rabbit'.

bb

ck

o

ck

Additional resources

Your pupil is now ready to use Set 3 of the Step by Step Reading Additional Resources. See the website or the accompanying instructions for details of how to use these.

Step 17

oo ee

moon
tree

You are now starting the second third of learning to read. Being able to sound out and read words of any length (one letter, one sound) is the first third. The second third is learning the sounds for which there is not a letter, and for which we use two or more letters called letter-groups. The final third is gaining fluency. Right up to the end of the book and for the rest of his life, however, your pupil will meet new words in which single letters will say their simple sound; even in a difficult word like 'rough' the 'r' sounds simply. As we learn new letter-groups, each one will give access to lots of new words, and we shall all the time keep coming back to words and spelling patterns that we have already met.

Explain that while our alphabet has 26 letters, in speech we use 44 sounds; that is, we have more sounds than letters. This problem is solved by using two or more letters together to make extra sounds. It is really very clever, and quite interesting, how letters work. (There is more than one way to spell some sounds but leave that for the moment. Do not make things become more complicated.)

Remind your pupil that each letter has a sound and a name (for example, 'hhh' and 'aitch'). Up until now you have been using the sounds of letters, but from now on when you are talking about letters, use their name: 'hhh' is the sound, 'aitch' is the name.

The first two new sounds are 'oo' and 'ee'. Say: 'One 'o' says 'o' (as in 'top') but two 'o's say 'oo' (as in 'moon'). Have your pupil repeat three times, 'Two 'o's says 'oo'". Then ask, 'What do two 'o's say?' Then 'If we want to write 'oo', what letters would we use?'

oo Explain how 'oo' can make a 'long' noise as in 'moon', 'cool', 'soon' etc, but also a shorter noise as in 'look', 'cook', 'book' etc.

oo		
moon	look
cool	cook
soon	book
room	good

ee The 'ee' is simpler. Say 'Two 'e's says 'eeee'.' Have your pupil repeat this three times, then have him read the 'ee' words in the list below.

ee		
tree	seem
feel	green
heel	see
week	bee

Point out that the words 'he' and 'we' rhyme with 'tree'.

Step 18

sh

fish

Remind your pupil that 'h' is the blowy letter. When you use it with another letter, you still blow – as in 'sh', 'ch' and 'th'. We first learn 'sh', the sound we make to tell people to hush. Have your pupil say 'sh', with his hand in front of his mouth, so that he can feel the wind of the blow. Have him say three times, "ess-aitch' says 'sh".

ship

fish

dish

brush

shop

Try this

A cook has a dish in his hand. He looks at a fish on a dish. His dish is too hot. He drops it. Crash! He drops his fish. Splash! He gets a brush and sweeps up his mess.

Exercise 18.1

Add 'sh' to complete these words.
Sound out the new words. Ask your teacher if you don't understand any of them.

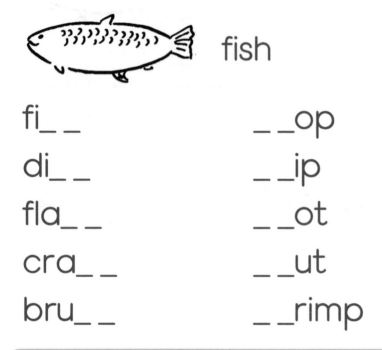 fish

fi_ _   _ _op

di_ _   _ _ip

fla_ _   _ _ot

cra_ _   _ _ut

bru_ _   _ _rimp

Try this

A man is in a shop. He sees a van crash into a tree. Smash! Sally sees it too. Andy runs from his shop. He has a camera. Flash. He shuts his shop and runs to get help.

Step 19

ch

chin

Read the 'sh' words from Step 18. Remind your pupil that 'h' is a blowy letter. With 'c', it makes a sound like a sneeze. Point out that 'sh' goes on longer, while 'ch' stops short. Have your pupil repeat three times, "See-aitch' says 'ch".

lunch
crunch
munch
chap
chop
chip

As your pupil practises writing 'ch' you may find it helpful to write a joined 'ch' in large letters with a yellow felt pen or highlighter, and let your pupil go over them, to get the feel of how you join the letters. Draw the letters separately, then add the joining bit in a different colour, to show the extra line. Write a large 'ch' in a pale colour, joined, and have your pupil go over it, to learn how to join the two letters.

Exercise 19.1

Add 'ch' to complete these words. Sound out the new words. Ask your teacher if you
don't understand any of them.

 chin

_ _ips   mu_ _   fet_ _

_ _op   su_ _   dit_ _

_ _ap   ri_ _   mat_ _

_ _in   crun_ _   scrat_ _

Point out that 'such', 'much' and 'rich' just end in 'ch', but other words with a short
vowel are spelt with 't-ch': 'patch', 'fetch', 'hitch', 'Scotch' and 'hutch'.

Try this

I munched on fish and chips for lunch. We had
lunch at a zoo. I munched my fish and chips on
a bench. We watched a chimp in a tree. He got
scratched by a branch.

Step 20

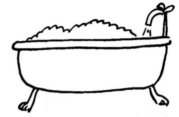

bath

Good speech helps good spelling. Remind your pupil that 'th' is another letter-group with an 'h' in it, so there will be a blow in the way you sound it. Tell your pupil that in 'th' the 't' stands for tongue so he should put the tip of his tongue out and then blow, to make the sound of 'th'.

Go back over a few pairs of letters: 't'/'d', 'p'/'b', 'k'/'g', and have your pupil put his hand on his throat, to feel that in the 't', 'p' and 'k' there is no tremble, but when we say 'd', 'b' and 'g' (in 'go'), our throat vibrates because the letters are voiced. For this to work the 't' must be just 't' and not 'ter', ('ter' is two sounds, 't' and 'er', and the 'er' is voiced.)

The letter-group 'th' can be both voiced (with tremble) and unvoiced. Have your pupil say 'bath', 'path' and 'with' with unvoiced 'th', then 'this', 'then' and 'that' with voiced 'th'.

For 'the' say, 'tee' 'aitch' 'ee' says 'the'.'

When your pupil sounds out 'bath', and realises its meaning, he may change it to 'bah...th' or 'barth', or to 'baff'. Explain that there is no such word as 'baff', and that for 'th' we must put out the tip of the tongue (think "t' for tongue, 'h' for blow'), but for 'f' we bite the bottom lip. Have the pupil say clearly 'deaf' and 'death'; 'free' and 'three'.

Try these

thin	think	tooth
this	thank	teeth
that	them	with
the	bath	

Exercise 20.1

Add 'th' to complete these words.

bath

_ _e   _ _ink   _ _en   pa_ _

_ _is   _ _em   wi_ _   _ _at

Exercise 20.2

Say the word from each picture on the opposite page. Listen to the word, and write its number in the chart below with the matching sound. Write one number in each space on the chart.

oo	ee	sh	ch	th

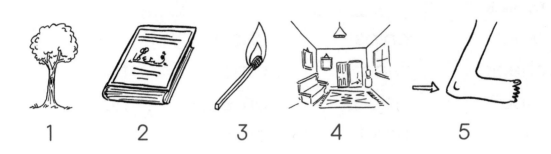

1   2   3   4   5

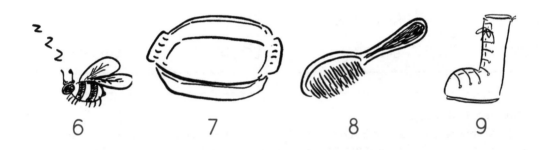

6   7   8   9

10   11   12

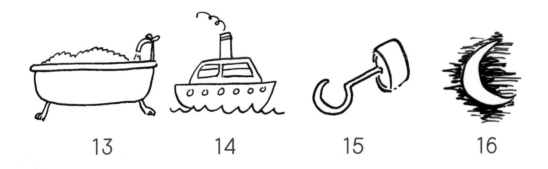

13   14   15   16

Try these

been	chips	chop	chunk
cheek	feed	fetch	fish
food	good	green	hood
look	much	pool	sheep
shop	sweet	shot	shut
ship	seem	spoon	teeth
tooth	sheets	tree	think
this	thick	that	week

Additional resources

Your pupil is now ready to use Set 4 of the Step by Step Reading Additional Resources. See the website or the accompanying instructions for details of how to use these.

Step 21

arm

The next five letter-groups are 'vowel + r'. The vowels are very important. Your pupil should now be using the names of the vowels, which are the long sounds:
'a' (ay)
'e' (ee)
'i' (I)
'o' (oh)
'u' (you)

When you sing the alphabet, you are singing the names of the letters. When we sound out we use letter-sounds. But when we talk about letters, we should now be using their names, occasionally reminding that "aitch' says 'hhh" and so on.

The letter-group 'ar' says the sound in 'car'. Pupils seem to find 'ar' and 'or' easier to learn than 'er', 'ir' and 'ur', which all make the same sound ('term', 'bird', 'curl'). If you wish to go slowly, do the 'ar' and 'or' first (Steps 21 - 22) and then the other three. If your pupil seems to be mopping it all up very easily, you can try all five together (Steps 21 - 23). Use your judgement.

ar When sounding the letter-group 'ar', the mouth is fairly wide open. Try to make the 'r' audible. Scottish reading attainment regularly comes out better than English, and I wonder if this is due to their clearer sound of the 'r'. Try to say 'carr' rather than 'cah'. Look in the mirror, and see if your lips move forward towards the end of the sound, as they should. Exaggerate the 'r' at the end for the next fortnight. Including words like 'sharp' emphasises to your pupil that letter-groups (like 'sh') once learned will be met again and again.

Exercise 21.1
Add 'ar' to complete these words. Then read each word out loud.

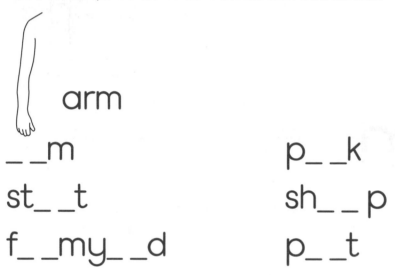

arm

_ _m   p_ _k

st_ _t   sh_ _p

f_ _my_ _d   p_ _t

Try this

A man plans to go to the farm. He starts his car and sets off to the farm. His dog barks at the sheep on the farm. He parks his car and tells his dog not to bark. The dog stops barking. Then he sets off to the market with his dog. He parks his car at the market and starts to shop. His dog sleeps in the car.

Step 22

or

fork

or For 'or' the mouth is not as wide open as for 'ar'. Again, try to sound the 'r' so that 'pour'/'pore' does not sound like 'paw'. 'Pouring' as in 'pouring with rain' should not sound the same as 'pawing' as in 'a cat pawing a mouse' (with no 'r' sound). (Try also 'soaring' and 'sawing'.)

Try these

fork	short
stork	lord
storm	ford
cork	porch
north	story

Exercise 22.1
Add 'or' to complete these words. Then read each word out loud.

fork

f_ _k   st_ _m
sh_ _t   c_ _n
m_ _ning   n_ _th
c_ _k

Try this

We had a storm this morning. It was a big storm.
It was so dark we needed a torch. We sat and
Rory told us a short story until the storm
ended.

Try these

charm	spark	smart	party
hardly	carpet	barn	target
sharp	farmyard	alarm	market
darling	north	corner	sport

lord   stork   horse   storm
morning   born   forget   cork
form   short   before   Norma
Gordon   porch   escort   Ford

Exercise 22.2
Add 'ar' to complete these words.

b _ _ n   c _ _   c _ _ ds
c _ _ pet   _ _ ch   st _ _
d _ _ t

Add 'or' to complete these words.

f _ _ k   st _ _ k   t _ _ ch
p _ _ ch   st _ _ m   h _ _ se
c _ _ k

Now write each of the words from Exercise 22.2 next to the correct picture below.

> **Additional resources**
>
> Your pupil is now ready to use Set 5 of the Step by Step Reading Additional Resources. See the website or the accompanying instructions for details of how to use these.

Step 23

er **ir** **ur**

er hammer

ir bird

ur church

The letter-groups 'er', 'ir', and 'ur' all sound the same. Look in the mirror to check that your lips come forward, and the sides of your mouth come in. The most common spelling for this sound is 'er', followed by 'ir' and then 'ur'. They are all easy to read, but we have to remember which to use for spelling. If you teach reading from sounds to letters, there will be about five choices for the long 'a' sound, with many dilemmas over which one to use. If you teach reading as this book does, from letters to sounds, there are dilemmas in the 'er' sound, 'ea', and homophones (like 'steel'/'steal'; 'there'/ 'their'), but you are on much surer ground than working from sounds to letters.

Exercise 23.1

Add the correct letter-group to complete these words.

hammer   bird   church

f _ _ n   sk _ _ t   f _ _
t _ _ m   sh _ _ t   b _ _ n
hamm _ _   g _ _ l   t _ _ n
butt _ _   b _ _ d   c _ _ l
fast _ _   th _ _ ty   h _ _ t
ladd _ _   f _ _ m   m _ _ m _ _
spann _ _   th _ _ st   sp _ _ t

Exercise 23.2

Practise saying the following words, and then write them beside the correct picture on the next two pages.

er	ir	ur
fern	shirt	church
river	blackbird	curls
hammer	skirt	nurse
ladder	thirty	burglar
finger	thirsty	turnip
swimmer	firm	purse
jumper		spurs
spanner		turkey

_____

_____

_____

_____

_____

_____

Exercise 23.3

Read these names:

Ernest	Bernadette	Robert
Albert	Herbert	Mervyn
Bernard	Hubert	Gertrude

Read the following words and explain what the people do:

gardener	carpenter	mender
farmer	hunter	shepherd

Comparatives and superlatives

Show how we make a comparative using '-er', and a superlative ending in '-est':

Positive	Comparative (+ 'er')	Superlative (+ 'est')
fast	faster	fastest
quick	quicker	quickest
long	longer	longest
strong	stronger	strongest
rich	richer	richest

Choose your words with care. Avoid 'wet' because the 't' has to be doubled in 'wetter' and 'wettest', and we have not yet taught doubling. Avoid 'wide', 'late', etc. because we have not yet taught what the 'e' does. Just say, for now, that in many words that end in '-er', the consonant in front is doubled:

hammer	spanner	better
letter	pepper	slipper
grasshopper	butter	

Try these

born	corner	card	bird
barn	burst	charm	corn
curl	dart	faster	father
fork	forty	firm	farm
fur	important	morning	jerk
murmur	nurse	person	shirt
skirt	sparkling	sport	term
thirty	thirsty	thorn	turn

Explain that 'father' is irregular in the way we say the 'a'.

And now this

A dog is faster than a sheep. The farmer has a dog to help with his herd of sheep. The farmer has a hammer. He gets his hammer and the wood and mends the sheep shelter. Then the sheep enter the shelter.

And this

A girl sits on a bench. She is thirsty. Her mum has a drink for her. She gives the drink to the girl. The girl turns to her mum and murmurs 'Thanks, Mum'.

Additional resources

Your pupil is now ready to use Set 6 of the Step by Step Reading Additional Resources. See the website or the accompanying instructions for details of how to use these.

Step 24

The next step is all about the way the letter 'e' works after a vowel. Step 17 showed that an 'e' after an 'e' (two 'e's) says 'ee', the sound of the name of the first vowel in the pair. This works for all the vowels, not just 'e'. Whenever a vowel is followed by an 'e' the vowel is long, that is it says its name ('ay', 'ee', 'I', 'oh' or 'you'). Thus:

'ae'   Mae (a Scottish name)
'ee'   tree
'ie'   pie
'oe'   toe
'ue'   value

This even works when a consonant separates the two vowels:

cake
theme
kite
hope
tune

Because 'e' can change the noise the vowels make in this way, we sometimes call it the 'magic 'e'' or, because we don't actually pronounce the 'e', the 'silent 'e''. The 'e' is silent at the end of English words.

Irregular words
Note that 'here' is regular but 'there' and 'where' are irregular.

Note that although the 'e' is silent at the end of English words, in some French words, such as 'café', the 'e' has an accent and is sounded. Where a word ends in two 'e's we do sound it: 'coffee', settee'.

Try these
Look at these words and check that the pupil notices whether there is a final 'e' or not.

cod ➜ code   fad ➜ fade

hop ➜ hope   tub ➜ tube

rat ➜ rate   them ➜ theme

pin ➜ pine   cub ➜ cube

Now look at these

cane	these	pine	toe
blue	shame	even	tune
open	clue	paper	Peter
fine	over	rescue	skate
concrete	wine	rope	tube
plate	extreme	tiger	stone
fumes	game	theme	wire
those	pure	gate	excuse

Exercise 24.1

Find the letter-groups in each word and read these words.

a - e	e - e	i - e	o - e	u - e
gate	even	pipe	rose	cube
cake	evening	wipe	nose	tube
game	these	ripe	hose	fumes
make	theme	stripes	those	use
spade	Steve	wine	rope	amuse
skates	concrete	time	hope	excuse
plate	Crete	tiger	stone	flute
paper	extreme	like	home	computer
same		tile	dome	refuse
fade		mine	Rome	included
cape		hide	hole	

Exercise 24.2

Add the correct vowels to complete these words.

a – e	i – e	o – e	u – e
r_k_	k_t_	n_s_	c_b_
g_t_s	sp_t_	r_s_	t_b_
sp_d_	d_v_	gl_b_	fl_t_
wh_l_	sl_d_	c_n_	
sn_k_	w_n_	b_n_	
	p_p_	tadp_l_	

Exercise 24.3

Write the correct word beside the following pictures.

So that earlier learning does not fade, it is time now to begin each lesson by revising earlier work. Before you begin each lesson, read through with your pupil a set of words from a step that you have already covered.

Try this

We go for a picnic with Peter. Peter takes a cake and his wife takes the plates. We like the food. We sit on a bench and look at the ducks. We feed the ducks. Then we make up a game. In the game Peter has to dive into the lake. He gets wet. It is late, and we go home.

Additional resources

Your pupil is now ready to use Set 7 of the Step by Step Reading Additional Resources. See the website or the accompanying instructions for details of how to use these.

Step 25

Doubling

Read through this section. You may decide to leave it until later for very young children aged three and four, but for older children and adults this section is very useful at this point as a way of making them consider letters/sounds and stop them guessing at meaning or predicting. This emphasises that reading is all about letters, a particular sequence of letters. We now know that the 'magic e' can jump back over one letter to make the previous vowel long. Thus rip becomes ripe, trip becomes tripe, etc.

The opposite of this is when we double a consonant to make (or keep) the preceding vowel short. Look at the following:

Hat (short 'a')
Hate (long 'a', because of magic 'e')
Hatted (i.e. wearing a hat; short 'a' because of double 't')

Pet (short 'e')
Pete (long 'e', because of magic 'e')
Petted (short 'e', because of double 't')

Strip (short 'i')
Stripe (long 'i', because of magic 'e')
Stripped (short 'i', because of double 'p')

Hop (short 'o')
Hope (long 'o', because of magic 'e')
Hopped (short 'o', because of double 'p')

> Remember to read through a set of words from an earlier step at the beginning of the lesson.

Comparatives and superlatives

Look at how this rule affects comparatives and superlatives:

wide	wider	widest
safe	safer	safest
fine	finer	finest

But:

fat	fatter	fattest
thin	thinner	thinnest
hot	hotter	hottest

When you need to double the 'c' sound ('c' or 'k'), to keep the vowel before it short, we use a 'k':

baker	packet	jacket	cricket
biker	lick	ticket	locket
joke	bucket	socket	suck

Remember that the rule about the magic 'e' applies to all vowels, not just 'e'. And remember that 'y' can be a vowel. Note the long vowel sounds in the words below on the left, and the short sounds on the right (after doubling):

pupil	puppet
holy	holly
acorn	accord

Note, also, that wherever a double consonant follows a vowel, the vowel is always short:

button	borrow	yellow
marry	merry	silly

Because 'i' works like the magic 'e', lengthening the vowel before it, when you add –ing to a word you drop the 'e'. You do not need both.

hop	hopping	hopped
hope	hoping	hoped
lick	licking	licked
like	liking	liked

Exercise 25.1

Try these:

Root word	-ing	-ed	-er
strip	str____	str____	str____
stripe	str____	str____	
mate	m____	m____	
rub	r____	r____	r____

Now try these. You have to decide whether to double the last consonant, drop the 'e', or make no change at all before adding the ending.

Root word	-ing	-ed
wipe	w_____	w_____
lick	l_____	l_____
stop	s_____	s_____
rust	r_____	r_____
bake	b_____	b_____

Step 26

-le

table

The next letter-group, '-le', follows on very easily after '-e' and doubling. This is the only other letter-group that does the same thing as 'e' (or any vowel), that is, it can jump back over one letter, but not two, to make a vowel say its name. Thus:

table	rabble
cradle	raffle
stable	dabble
Keble	pebble
trifle	little
noble	gobble
bugle	struggle

Remember to read through a set of words from an earlier step at the beginning of each lesson.

Lots of words end in '-le', but in most of them the vowel sound is short (as in 'battle', 'settle', 'little', 'bottle' and 'struggle'). This is because in all of these words there are two consonants before the 'le', so the 'magic' effect of the 'le' does not work.

When the letters between the vowel and the '-le' are 'st', the vowel is short and the 't' is silent.

castle*

pestle

whistle

jostle

rustle

(*Of course, although the 'a' of castle should be short, many people pronounce 'castle' as 'cahsle' with a long 'a'.)

Finally, note that 'le' only works its magic on the vowel in words of two syllables. In longer words, the vowel remains short.

miracle	possible
obstacle	terrible
oracle	visible
spectacles	breakable
particle	tolerable

Teaching how the letters work helps to keep attention on letters, sequence, direction and sounds and off illustrations, which can distract. This stage should be short and easy. Do not wait until your pupil can spell every word before moving on.

Try these

apple	battle	crackle	castle
handle	pebble	settle	thimble
little	middle	tremble	simple
twinkle	whistle	bottle	uncle
cuddle	jungle	purple	puzzle
struggle	snuggle	terrible	rustle
possible	title	thistle	table
feeble	rifle	noble	Bible

Try this

I left the horses in the stable. I took the saddles and put them in the middle of the table. Then I took an apple from the tree to feed to the horses. But my hands were hot and I was not able to feed the horses. My hands were hot and I dropped the apple. The horses jostled me in the stable. The horses had tangled manes. But I had to get them an apple, and I went to get help.

Exercise 26.1

Complete the following words and write the numbers by the correct picture.

1. app_ _   7. bott_ _

2. bang_ _   8. cand_ _

3. padd_ _   9. hand_ _

4. fidd_ _   10. rectang_ _

5. thimb_ _   11. dimp_ _

6. kett_ _   12. scribb_ _

Additional resources

Your pupil is now ready to use Set 8 of the Step by Step Reading Additional Resources. See the website or the accompanying instructions for details of how to use these.

soap

When 'oa' are found together, they always behave the same way.
'When these two vowels go walking, the first one does the talking'.

So, get your pupil to repeat three times, "o-a' says 'Oh!". Thus:

boat

soap

road

coat

Note, however, that when 'r' follows a vowel or vowels, their sound changes. 'Oa'+ 'r' sounds like 'or'. If you sound out 'oa-r', you almost have two syllables, which we do not want, so teach your pupil to say "oh-r' says 'or".

Remember to read through a set of words from an earlier step at the beginning of each lesson.

Exercise 27.1
Add the correct letter-group to complete these words.

 oa

soap	r_ _d	g_ _l
fl_ _t	s_ _k	thr_ _ t
b_ _t	c_ _t	m_ _n
c_ _l	gr_ _n	c_ _st
J_ _n	r_ _st	f_ _l
t_ _st	l_ _f	

 oar

boar	b_ _ _d
h_ _ _d	s_ _ _

Try these

The boat floated on the river. The boat was
made of oak. The man in the boat wore a red
coat and spoke with a croak, like a goat.

Step 28

Teach your pupil the sounds that 'ai' and 'oi' make. Teach him that sometimes 'i' becomes 'y', but the sound stays the same. Thus:

sail   tray   playing

coin   boy   boiling

Words ending in 'i'

No English word ends in 'q', 'u', 'v', 'j' or 'i'.

We do use some words that end in 'i', but they are not English:

      'ski' is a Norwegian word;

      'spaghetti', 'macaroni' and 'broccoli' are Italian;

      'taxi' is half of 'taxicab' (we say 'taxi', the Americans say 'cab').

In the word 'I', i is the beginning, middle and end.

Words ending in 'y'

If a word ends in 'y', look carefully at what happens when we add extra letters to the end of the word: the 'y' changes into an 'i'. This works whether the 'y' is long or short.

Remember to read through a set of words from an earlier step at the beginning of each lesson.

Adjectives:

happy   happily   happier   happiest   happiness

Verbs:

hurry   hurries   hurried   hurrying*
worry   worries   worried   worrying*

*We cannot have two 'i's together, except in a non-English word such as 'skiing'.

And the long 'i' sound:

cry   cries   cried   crying
reply   replies   replied   replying

Nouns

pony   ponies
cherry   cherries
fly   flies

This works whether the word is adjective, noun or verb, and whether the 'y' is long or short. You cannot have 'i' at the end of a word, but you can have 'y' anywhere. At the beginning of a word or syllable, 'y' is a consonant (e.g. 'yes', 'beyond'). Elsewhere it is a vowel, making the same sounds as 'i'.

Exercise 28.1
Add 'y' to complete these words.
'Y' saying the short sound:

funny   p_jamas   sill_

p_ramid   s_stem   s_rup

famil_   m_ster_   m_th

d_slexia

'Y saying the long sound:

h_drant   def_   satisf_

den_   d_namite   repl_

multipl_   p_thon   verif_

d_namo

'r'-controlled 'ai'

Vowels change their sound when followed by an 'r' (see Step 27). We say they are 'r'-controlled. When 'r' follows 'ai', the sound changes slightly. 'Air', 'chair' and 'fair' should be one syllable and not 'ay-er'. Once the pupil gets used to 'air', it will be easily read in other words.

Irregular words
Note that 'oir' is rare; 'choir' is pronounced 'kwire', and is an irregular word.
In 'said', the spelling is regular; it is the pronunciation that is irregular.

Try these

aim	chair	nail	railway
entertain	explain	maintain	obtain
pain	rain	train	strain
holiday	play	Thursday	stray
Sunday	pray	tray	Ray
noise	spoil	point	join
foil	coin	boil	coil
boy	enjoy	annoy	

Exercise 28.2

Practise saying these words:

ai	ay	oi	oy
sail	tray	coin	boy
aim	play	boil	toy
nails	pray	spoil	enjoy
hair	Sunday	joint	annoy
upstairs	holiday	toilet	oyster
explain	spray	point	destroy
exclaim	crayon		

Exercise 28.3

Write the correct word next to each picture. Each word contains 'ai', 'ay', 'oi' or 'oy'.

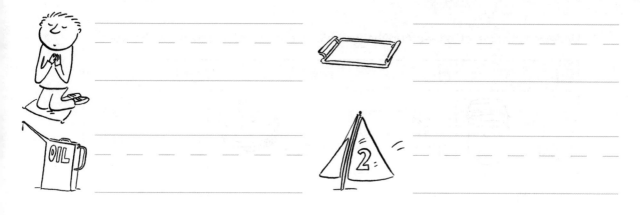

Exercise 28.4

Add the correct letter-group to complete each word and then say the word. Ask if you do not understand the meaning.

ai	ay	oi	oy
paint	tray	coin	boy
tr_ _n	cl_ _	f_ _l	t_ _
p_ _d	p_ _	sp_ _l	R_ _
l_ _d	l_ _	p_ _nt	enj_ _
s_ _d*	s_ _	b_ _l	ann_ _

* Note how the spelling of this word is regular; it is the pronunciation which is irregular.

Underline the correct letter-group that completes each word and then say the word.

ai	ay	oi	oy
paint	tray	coin	boy
again	play	joint	destroy
afraid	spray	toilet	employ
explain	away	noise	oyster
obtain	may	appoint	royal
maintain	display	poison	loyal
fail	holiday	avoid	coy
nail	hay	moist	

Exercise 28.5

Read these words, then write each one in the correct column in the table opposite. Write the words without copying if you can. Ask the meaning of any new words.

boy	chain	toy	hay
nail	boiling	spray	waiter
snail	tail	saint	trailer
coin	train	pointing	oil-can
pray	tray	paint-brush	rain
coil	royalty	oyster	railway
joint	paid	fray	play
layer	destroy		

ai	ay	oi	oy

Additional resources

Your pupil is now ready to use Set 9 of the Step by Step Reading Additional Resources.
See the website or the accompanying instructions for details of how to use these.

Step 29

ea

sea
bread
steak

Letter-groups that are consistent and reliable are easier to learn. We can say 's-h' says 'sh' and it will, every time (except in the words 'mis-hap' and 'mis-hit', which are not much used by new readers). However, 'ea' is not consistent. There are many words in which 'ea' says the same sound as 'ee', many others where it says the short 'e' sound as in 'head' and others where it makes the long 'a' sound as in 'great'.

Remember to read through a set of words from an earlier step at the beginning of each lesson.

When your pupil meets words using the letter-group 'ea', ask him to try the 'ee' sound first; if that does not produce a real word, try the short 'e' and then the long 'a'. For example, for 'peas' the long 'ee' works; for 'steady' try 'steedy', which is not a word, so try 'steddy', which is the sound; for 'steak' try 'steek', then 'stek' before finding the correct sound. There is no rule as to which is which. Just to make life difficult, in a few words the same letters give different-sounding words:

Can you read it?   I have read it.

A lead pencil.   Lead the way.

Exercise 29.1
Add the correct letter-group to complete these words.

ea (ee)	ea (short e)	ea (long a)
sea	bread	steak
b_ _ch	h_ _ven	gr_ _t
p_ _ch	h_ _d	br_ _k
str_ _m	st_ _dy	
app_ _r	w_ _ther	

'r'-controlled 'ea'

You have already learned that the five vowels and the letter-group 'ai' all change their sound when followed by an 'r'. We say they are 'r'-controlled. The letter-group 'ea' can also be 'r'-controlled, producing three different sounds:

1. In four words, 'ear' sounds like 'air':

bear	pear
wear	tear

2. In a few words, 'ear' sounds like 'er':

earn	learn
early	earth
search	pearl
heard	

3. In two words, 'ear' sounds like 'ar':

heart	hearth

4. In other words, 'ear' sounds the same as 'eer':

ear	year
fear	dear
appear	

Try these

please	reason	steal	leave
clean	meat	dear	feast
least	fear	breathe	near
year	teach	appear	easy
deaf	bread	dreadful	ready
jealous	thread	steady	tread
weather	feather	instead	heavy

Exercise 29.2
Add 'ea' to complete these words, and then write each word beside the correct picture.

j_ _ns   p_ _k   sp_ _r

m_ _t   str_ _m   sw_ _ter

_ _gle   br_ _d   b_ _ds

thr_ _d   sh_ _rs   b_ _rd

s_ _   s_ _t   t_ _pot

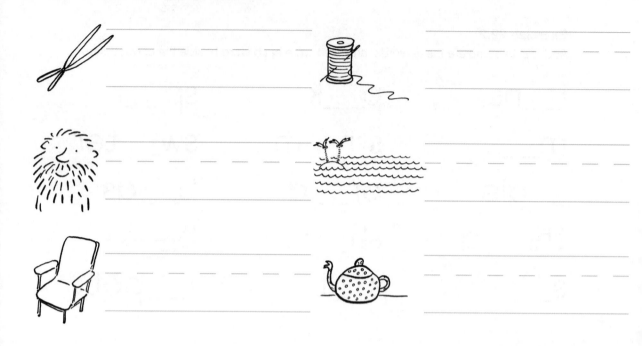

Try this

My brother eats a lot of meat. But at breakfast
he eats toast or bread. For a treat I like to have
steak and a pear or a peach.

Additional resources

Your pupil is now ready to use Set 10 of the Step by Step Reading Additional Resources.
See the website or the accompanying instructions for details of how to use these.

Step 30

Soft c g

This step may take some time to cover.

The pupil has by now had a lot of practice in making a 'c' say 'kuh', and a 'g' say its hard sound as in 'go'; but he has also met 'ch' as in 'chop'. The letters 'c' and 'g' are the only two in the alphabet that can be either hard or soft. The sound we learned first, as in 'cat' and 'dog', is the hard sound. The soft sound is the sound 'ee' we hear in 'celery' and 'jee' in 'germ'.

They say this soft sound when followed by 'e', 'i' or 'y'. This gives us six letter-groups: 'ce', 'ci', 'cy', 'ge', 'gi', 'gy'. You can either take them one at a time, or explain the general principle and let your pupil try out all six.

When soft 'c' and 'g' are introduced, some learners try to change every 'c' and 'g' into the new, soft sound. Tell your pupil that all the words where 'c' and 'g' have previously said the hard sound will remain the same, that we are not changing any words we have met already but are looking at new words.

You can join the two letters, 'ce', 'ci', 'cy' etc together by writing them next to one another (in joined-up writing) if you wish. This may help to imprint on your pupil's mind that they go together.

Remember to read through a set of words from an earlier step at the beginning of each lesson.

Soft 'c'

ce	ci	cy
fence	pencil	cylinder
dance advance necessary December	city decide excited scissors	fancy Nancy Cyril bicycle

Note the very odd word 'once', formed from the equally odd word 'one'. Irregular words like this just have to be learnt.

Double 'c'
When you have 'cc' before 'a', 'o' or 'u', it says 'k':

accost   accord   accustom

When you have 'cc' before 'e', 'i' or 'y' (the letters that make 'c' soft), the first 'c' says 'k', and the second 'c' says 's', so that 'cc' sounds like 'x':

succeed   success   accept
accent   access   accelerate

Note that Dixon and Dickson sound the same.

Look out for '-cess' in words, as this helps to remind you when to use 'cc' and when to use 'ss':

access   success   princess
recess   abscess   necessary

When to use 'c', 'k' and 'ck'

At the beginning of a word, the 'k' sound before 'a', 'o' or 'u' uses the letter 'c':

cat   cot   cut

but before 'e', 'i' or 'y' it is 'k' (because 'ce', 'ci' and 'cy' would make the 'c' say the the 's' sound):

kettle   kitten   Kylie

In a word of more than one syllable ending in the sound 'ick', it is spelt 'ic':

panic   picnic   frantic

mimic   logic   magic

fantastic   Atlantic   Pacific

arithmetic

After a long vowel, the 'k' sound is 'k':

bake   like   stoke

duke   week   peak

steak

The letter-group 'ck' follows a short vowel in words of one syllable like:

pack   peck   pick

rock   duck

Point out to your pupil that he is learning how letters work together. This benefits his reading and, of course, his spelling.

Exercise 30.1

Find the correct letter-group in each word that completes these words, and then sound them out. Find out the meaning of any new words.

ce	-ce	-nce	ci	cy
centre	face	dance	city	icy
accept	space	glance	cider	Nancy
except	grace	once	citrus	chancy
cent	lace	France	pencil	mercy
process	recent	mince	decide	leniency
access	decent	since	excited	literacy
success	twice	princess	circle	fancy
succeed	price	concert	circus	cyst
century	mice	licence	cinema	cyril
certain	rice		scissors	Cynthia
ascend	ocean		racing	cyanide
descend	grocer		icing	cyclone
force	police		incident	cypress
cement	reduce		cinders	bicycle
conceal	notice			

Now try these

electricity	necessary	accident
ambulance	emergency	arrogance
difference	advance	sentence
pretence	insistence	distance
medicine	decency	democracy

Exercise 30.2

Why are the following words spelt the way they are?

lack	lake	lace	lacking	lacing
lick	like	lice	licking	liking
duck	duke		ducking	
trick	trike	trice	tricking	pricing
prick		rice	pricking	
	make	mace		making

Soft 'g'

Just as 'c' is soft in front of 'e', 'i' and 'y', so is 'g'. Thus:

German   gin   gym

My father's first name was George. All my life, until I learned the rule about 'ge',
I wondered why his name had such an odd spelling. I learned this rule when I was 48.
So you are way ahead of me!

In a word like 'age', the first vowel has an 'e' two letters later, so the first vowel is long:

Regent   digest   huge

The same thing is found with 'ce':

face   recent   grocer

If you want a short vowel in front of 'ge', instead of putting two 'g's (except in 'suggest' and 'exaggerate') we put '-dge':

badge	hedge	bridge
lodge	smudge	

This is voiced.

The unvoiced equivalent is '-tch':

patch	fetch	witch
Scotch	Dutch	

Irregular words

Surprisingly, it is the following simple words that are irregular:

rich	much	such
which	duchess	

This may be a good time to point out that printed material often shows 'g' as 'ɡ'.

Try these

accept	ambulance	bicycle
change	city	danger
December	digital	excellent
except	face	fancy
garage	general	giant
ginger	grocer	hedge
huge	ice	imagine
necessary	police	princess
scarcely*	suggest	sponge

*Note the 'ar' in 'scarcely' does not sound as in 'car', but sounds like 'air'. This is a very tricky word.

Words ending in '-nge'

Many words end in '-nge'. When '-nge' follows 'e', 'i', 'o' or 'u' the vowel is short (as in 'hinge'), but 'a' is different. In orange the 'a' sounds like 'i'. In other words, the 'a' is usually long:

range	ranger	change
danger	stranger	mange
manger	angel	

Words ending in '-age'

Many words end in '-age'. The word 'age' has a long, clear 'ay' sound. When the '-age' is the ending of a longer two-syllable word, we do not say it as a clear '-age'. It sounds more like '-idge'. You could say each word first with a long 'a' ('vill-ay-j'... 'vill-idge'):

village	cabbage	image
bandage	postage	garage
manage	package	damage

In 'barrage', 'garage', 'camouflage' and 'sabotage', with the 'a' making the sound we hear in 'lard', we use more of a French pronunciation.

Exercise 30.3

Add 'ge' to complete these words and then say each word. Then for the first 12 words, find the matching picture on the next pages and write the word beside it.

ca_ _	pa_ _	hin_ _
bad_ _	sled_ _	cotta_ _
_ _ms	oran_ _s	bad_ _r
brid_ _	an_ _l	banda_ _
dan_ _r	dun_ _on	

hu_ _   mana_ _   cabba_ _
villa_ _   gara_ _   passa_ _
jud_ _   lar_ _   dama_ _
fud_ _   spon_ _   chan_ _
_ _ntle   Geor_ _   sur_ _on
a_ _   ra_ _   sta_ _
wa_ _   frin_ _

Exercise 30.4

Find the correct letter-group in each word.

-tch	-dge	ge	-nge
witch	badge	huge	fringe
hatch	edge	wage	hinge
scratch	ledge	large	plunge
stretch	hedge	urgent	sponge
hitch	bridge	George	orange
pitch	sludge	regent	change
stitch	fudge	digest	danger
ditch	judge	Nigel	angel
Dutch	grudge	gentle	stranger
clutch	nudge	suggest	ranger

In most '–ange' words, the 'a' is long.

Exercise 30.5

Fill in the letter-groups and read the words.

-age	gi	gy
rage	engine	gymnastics
man___	tra__c	aller__
vill___	ima__ne	E__pt
dam___	__raffe	ener__
cabb___	__nger	biolo__
band___	__ant	zoolo__
sav___	re__ster	ornitholo__
pass___	en__ne	sociolo__
im___	di__tal	geolo__
lugg___	a__tate	criminolo__
post___	__gantic	bacteriolo__

In words of more than one syllable, '-age' sounds like '–idge'.

Exercise 30.6
More practice at letter-groups

gi	gy	ce
giraffe	gymnastics	face
engine	Egypt	fence
digital	zoology	pence
magic	biology	dice
tragic	energy	price
giant	allergy	slice
imagine		laces
ginger		scent

-nce	ci	cy
dance	pencil	cylinder
advance	cigarette	fancy
glance	scissors	Nancy
France	decide	bicycle
ambulance	excited	Cyril
distance	circle	cyclone
difference	city	cygnet
since	precious	

Now write the correct word next to the correct picture. They all come from the lists in
Excercise 30.6.

By now you may have started the pupil on reading books, or have encouraged him gradually to read more and more of the words that you know he can read when you read together. Let your pupil read any books with large print, just helping with words that have letter-groups not yet taught, or irregular words. Use your judgement.

Additional resources

Your pupil is now ready to use Set 11 of the Step by Step Reading Additional Resources. See the website or the accompanying instructions for details of how to use these.

Try these

I cycled to the cinema once. I cycled along a path made of cement. The film was a huge success. The main actor danced and had a Scottish accent.

Step 31

gu

guitar

Sometimes we want a hard 'g' in front of 'e', 'i' or 'y'. To prevent the 'g' being softened by the 'e', 'i' or 'y' we need to add a letter to keep them apart. We do this with a 'u' which forms a wall between the 'g' and the 'e', 'i' or 'y'. Thus:

guitar   guess

guide   guest

There is a 'u' in the word 'guard', a 'u' that is not really needed. Compare it with 'regard'. Note also that the West Indian island Antigua is pronounced 'Antee-ga' not 'Antig-ew-a'.

Remember to read through a set of words from an earlier step at the beginning of each lesson.

Exercise 31.1
Add 'gu' to complete these words.

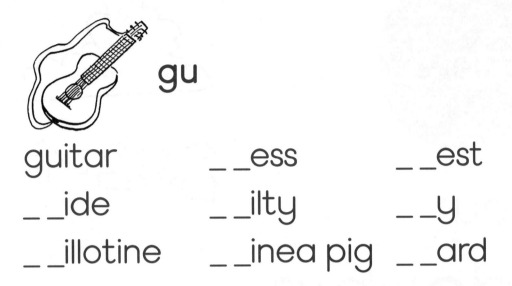

gu

guitar   _ _ess   _ _est

_ _ide   _ _ilty   _ _y

_ _illotine   _ _inea pig   _ _ard

Try this

I have a guest coming this weekend. She is a girl guide called Ginny. Her father is a guard on the railway. Her father feels guilty when he goes to the railway and is not at home to help with her guitar.

Step 32

ou

double

The letter-group 'ou' can make at least five sounds and 'ow' can make two.

'ou' can make the short sound in words such as:

double   trouble   nourish

'ou' can make the long sound in words such as:

south   around   count

> Remember to read through a set of words from an earlier step at the beginning of each lesson.

'ou' can say 'oo' in words such as:

you   youth   group

soup   coupon   route

routine

'ou' says short 'u' in words ending in '-ous':

famous   curious   precious

spacious   delicious   avaricious

'our' sounds like 'or':

pour   four

'ou' also changes its sound in the 'ough' words (see Step 37).

Try this

My cousin and I live in a house. Last week we made a cake. A mouse ran past us on the ground. My cousin shouted loudly at the mouse and I dropped the cake.

Exercise 32.1
Add the correct letter-group to complete these words.

ou	ou (silent o)
cloud	$2 \times 2 = 4$ double
sh_ _t	n_ _rish
ar_ _nd	c_ _ntry
s_ _th	c_ _sin
c_ _nt	fam_ _s
tr_ _sers	curi_ _s

Step 33

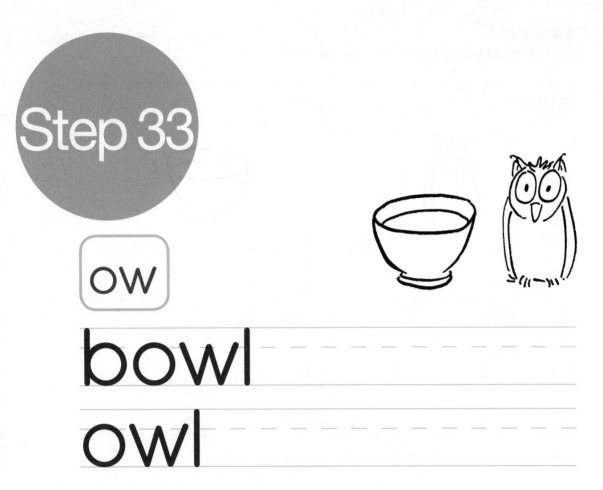

ow

bowl

owl

The letter-group 'ow' can say two sounds. It can say the long 'o' sound in 'bowl' and the sound it says in words such as 'owl', 'towel' and 'cow'.

Remember to read through a set of words from an earlier step at the beginning of each lesson.

Exercise 33.1

Add the correct letter-group to complete these words.

ow	ow
owl	bowl
c_ _	sl_ _
t_ _n	sn_ _
cr_ _d	gr_ _
p_ _der	pill_ _
n_ _	borr_ _
h_ _	yell_ _

Exercise 33.2

Say these words aloud. Then write them next to the correct picture on the following pages.

owl   fountain   mouth

cow   bow   arrow

house   mower   elbow

flower   pound   mouse

pillow   cloud   towel

shower

and

Exercise 33.3

See if you can find the correct letter-group used in these words.

ou	ou	ow	ow
mouse	double	cow	mower
out	trouble	owl	snow
shout	couple	town	grow
about	country	down	show
ground	cousin	drown	throw
sound	nourish	powder	pillow
pound	encourage	shower	yellow
south	young	flower	sorrow
mouth	furious	crowd	arrow
house	famous	towel	flow
trousers	delicious	clown	borrow
count	ferocious	tower	

Try these

I live in a very crowded town. It keeps growing and seems to be eating up all the country around it. If I look out of my window I cannot see any flowers. Most of the birds have flown away. This makes me sad and I frown or shout aloud.

Step 34

 **au** **aw**

haunt

saw

These two letter-groups say the same sound, and are very reliable. Very few words end in 'u' so words that have the 'au' sound at the end use the ending 'aw' instead such as 'straw', 'paw' etc.

Remember to read through a set of words from an earlier step at the beginning of each lesson.

Try this

Paul lives in a haunted house. He is a nautical man and goes to sea in a trawler. His wife works in a laundry. She has a cat with big claws. The cat likes raw fish.

Exercise 34.1

Add either 'au' or 'aw' to complete these words.

au	aw
haunted	saw
P_ _l	p_ _
_ _gust	cl_ _
bec_ _se	l_ _
l_ _ndry	str_ _
_ _tomatic	cr_ _l
l_ _nch	y_ _n

Additional resources

Your pupil is now ready to use Set 12 of the Step by Step Reading Additional Resources. See the website or the accompanying instructions for details of how to use these.

Step 35

gh   ght

light

Our beautiful language is made up of words from many other languages. When the Vikings came over, their language contained a sound in the back of the throat, a guttural that the Anglo-Saxons could not pronounce. This sound was marked by the letters 'gh', but as the Anglo-Saxons couldn't pronounce this sound, the letters 'gh' often make no sound, as in 'light', 'fight' and 'might'. It may help to remember that 'in '-gh' words the 'gh' has gone home'.

Remember to read through a set of words from an earlier step at the beginning of each lesson.

A	B	C	D	E	F
G	H	I	J	K	L
M	N	O	P	Q	R
S	T	U	V	W	X
Y	Z				

y	s	m	g	a
z	t	n	h	b
	u	o	i	c
	v	p	j	d
	w	q	k	e
	x	r	l	f

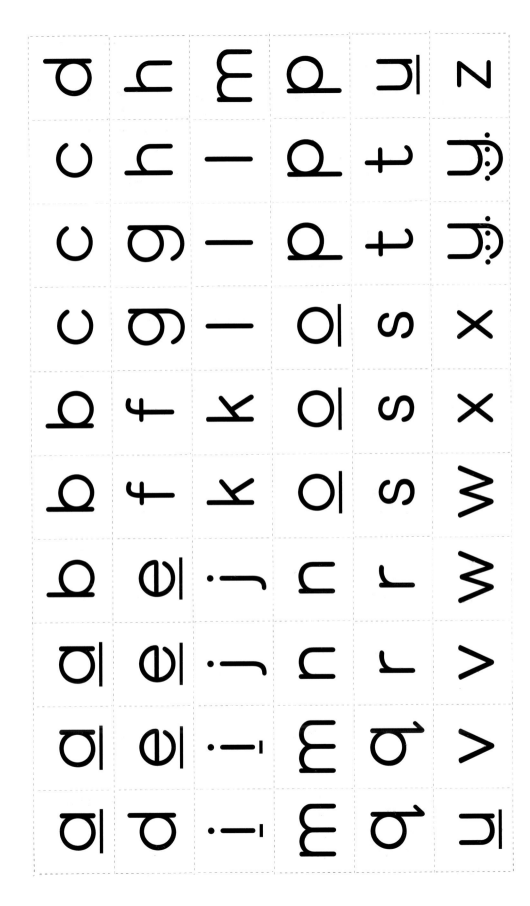

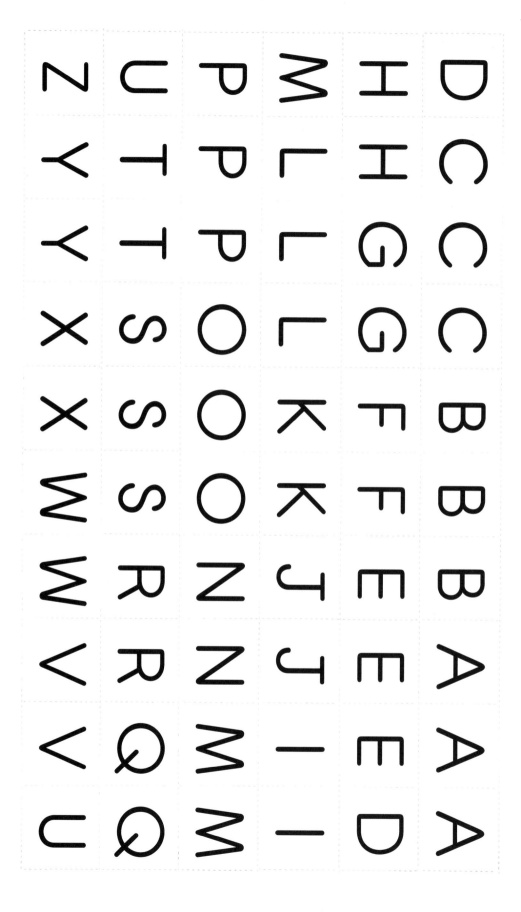

Exercise 35.1
Add 'gh' to complete these words.

 light

si_ _t	fi_ _t	bri_ _t
ni_ _t	ti_ _t	fli_ _t
fri_ _t	mi_ _t	ri_ _t

Note also:
The 'gh' is silent in the following:

sigh	high	weight
eight	weigh	neigh
neighbour	sleigh	deign
reign		

Try this

At eight o'clock last night some men had a fight. The police caught them. One man shouted but his daughter began to cry and the neighbours got a fright. 'It is not right to fight at night' they shouted.

Step 36

ought   aught

fought

Words containing 'ought' and 'aught' obey the rule we learnt in Step 35 in that the 'gh' remains silent. But now we need to look at the effect 'gh' can have on the vowel sounds 'ou' and 'au'. Note that 'ought' sounds the same as 'aught'.

ought	caught	bought	taught
brought	daughter	fought	nought
thought	slaughter		

However, in some words the 'gh' in 'augh' makes the sound of the letter 'f':

laugh   laughter

In the next step we will see what can happen to words ending in '-ough'

Remember to read through a set of words from an earlier step at the beginning of each lesson.

Step 37

-ough

You have already met 'ough' followed by 't', in words such as 'fought' and 'bought'. But where a word ends in '-ough', without the 't', it becomes a lot harder. We cannot say, as we have done previously, "ough' says ...' because it says six different things, in addition to the way it sounds in the 'ought' words.

This is the group of words from which people choose when they want to try to prove that phonics does not work. Over 90 per cent of words are regular, however, and by concentrating on what is regular within words (the 'r' in 'rough', the 'thr' in 'through'), phonics helps pupils to cope with the irregularities.

Remember to read through a set of words from an earlier step at the beginning of each lesson.

The six different 'ough' sounds:

	the **ough** says
cough trough	**off**
enough rough tough	**uff**
plough bough	**ow** as in 'cow'
through (and only in this word)	**oo**
dough although	'Oh!', the long sound of the vowel **o**
thoroughly borough Scarborough	**u** as in 'cup'

Get your pupil to read the words above in the first column, first with the help of the pronunciation clues, then without, from top to bottom, then bottom to top, then randomly. Finally dictate the words to your pupil and see if he can write them down correctly.

Exercise 37.1
Fill in the gaps in the sentences below using these words.

cough	trough	enough	rough
plough	bough	through	dough
thorough	borough	although	

1. Billy _____ed all _____ the night; he could not get _____ sleep, _____ he did take his medicine.

2. The pig ate from a _____ under the _____ of a tree.

3. The farmer _____ed his field _____ly.

4. The _____ was in an inner city, with a lot of _____ boys.

5. The baker mixed _____ before he made bread.

Step 38

wa   qua

was

The letter-group 'wa' hardly ever says the sound in 'wax' or 'waggle'; and 'qua' only sounds like 'qua' in the word 'quack'! Most of the time 'wa' sounds like 'wo', and 'qua' sounds like 'kwo'.

want	watch	wasp
quarrel	quality	squash

The best way to deal with the remaining letter-groups 'war' and 'quar' is by completing the words in a column, pronouncing them correctly and checking that your pupil knows what they mean.

Remember to read through a set of words from an earlier step at the beginning of each lesson.

Exercise 38.1

Find the correct letter-groups used in these words and then read them out. Ask for the meaning of any you do not know.

wa	war	qua	quar
was	warm	quarrel	quart
want	warning	quarry	quarter
wash	warden	quality	quartz
watch	reward	squash	
wasp	backward	squabble	
waffle	forwards	squadron	
wand	towards	quarantine	
swan			
swallow			

Try this

I was wallowing in the warm pool until my dogs jumped in to wash in the water. The water in the warm pool turned brown and the quality of the water went from bad to worse.

Exercise 38.2

Say the words, then write them beside the correct picture.

wand   watch   wasp

swan   swallow

Step 39

wh

when

In the following question words beginning with 'wh', the 'h' is sounded and not silent:

what?	when?	which?
where?	why?	whether
whither?		

Show your pupil how to write a question mark, and explain how it is used with questions. Show him how we use the pitch of our voice to mark a question when we are speaking, and use a question mark when we are writing.

Irregular words
Note that 'who' is irregular.

Long vowels in short words:

Now is a good time to show your pupil the folowing short words where the vowels say their long sound:

my	fly	cry
why	try	fry
shy	spy	dry
sky		

or say their name:

sold	so	he
bold	no	we
gold	go	be
cold	Lo!	· me
fold		
hold		
told		

Exceptions include:

to	who	do

Try this

What did he say? When will they come back? Which one is best? Where did they go? Why did they have to go away? Did they say whether they were coming back?

Step 40

al

In a few words, 'al' says 'aw'.

Exercise 40.1
Add 'al' to complete these words.

all	ball	c_ _l
t_ _l	st_ _l	sm_ _l
h_ _l	f_ _l	w_ _l
_ _ter	w_ _k	t_ _k
ch_ _k	st_ _k	h_ _t
m_ _t	s_ _t	b_ _d
sc_ _d	_ _so	_ _most
_ _ways	_ _together	

Remember to read through a set of words from an earlier step at the beginning of each lesson.

Exercise 40.2
Write each of these words next to the correct picture.

straw   lawn   paw

ball   draw   gauntlet

sauce   wall

Try this

My parents are very tall. I am very small. When we go for walks I have to jog to keep up. One day I will fall over.

Step 41

wor

worm

'Wor' says 'wer'.

Exercise 41.1
Add 'wor' to complete these words.

_ _ _d   _ _ _ld   _ _ _k

_ _ _th   _ _ _se   _ _ _st

Remember to read through a set of words from an earlier step at the beginning of each lesson.

Step 42

Words of French origin

In words that come from French:

'i' sounds like 'ee'. ('-ine', 'igne', 'ique').
For example:

magazine   marine   trampoline

'ch' sound like 'sh'.
For example:

chef   machine

The endings '-que' and '-gue' sound like 'k' and (hard) 'g'.
For example:

cheque   antique
vague   vogue

Remember to read through a set of words from an earlier step at the beginning of each lesson.

Exercise 42.1

Find the correct letter-group used in these words and then read them out.

-ine	ch	-que	-gue
machine	chef	cheque	catalogue
Pauline	machine	antique	dialogue
marine		unique	fatigue
margarine		picturesque	league
guillotine		grotesque	intrigue
magazine			vague
tangerine			vogue
nectarine			rogue
trampoline			

Try this

The catalogue says the hotel has a good chef.
He always uses butter rather than margarine.
He prefers nectarines to tangerines. There are
lots of antiques in the hotel. You can buy these
and you can pay by cheque.

Step 43

The long sound of u

Look at the words on the opposite page. Your pupil has already learned the first two ways of spelling the long sound of 'u', as in 'value' (using 'ue') and 'cube' (using 'u' + magic 'e'). The third column of words on the next page is similar to this, reminding us that *any* vowel two letters after a 'u' can make the 'u' say its name. The fourth column is 'ui', with only about half a dozen words, and finally 'ew'.

To distinguish 'blew' from 'blue', make the connection with the 'w' ('ow', 'ew'), that 'blow' and 'blew' go together, as do 'grow' and 'grew'; 'throw' and 'threw' (not through).

Try this

The sky was bright blue today and the weather was very humid. We picked some tulips and sang a happy tune. We threw a ball through the air but I fell and bruised myself. I sat down until my mum came to the rescue, singing a merry tune. We looked at the view and then joined the queue to go home.

Remember to read through a set of words from an earlier step at the beginning of each lesson.

Exercise 43.1

Read the words below to find the correct letter-group.

ue	u – e	– u –	ui	ew
glue	cube	music	suit	screw
blue	tube	pupil	fruit	few
clue	tune	uniform	recruit	new
cue	fumes	union	pursuit	stew
value	cure	tulip	juice	grew
tissue	acute	humid	bruise	threw
statue	student	usual	cruise	blew
rescue	use	gradual		flew
avenue	amuse	peculiar		steward
queue	excuse	stupid		view
pursue	duke	duty		review
				pew

Words of Greek origin

Another language from which we get many words is Greek. In these words, 'ph' says 'f', and 'ch' says 'k'.
For example:

photo	physics	graph
chorus	chord	school

Also note that 'ps' was a single letter in Greek. Words beginning with 'ps' sound as if the 'p' was not there.
For example:

psychotic	psalm

> Remember to read through a set of words from an earlier step at the beginning of each lesson.

Exercise 44.1

Add the correct letter-group to complete these words.

ph	ch
dolphin	school
ele_ _ant	e_ _o
or_ _an	_ _emist
_ _ilip	an_ _or
ne_ _ew	_ _ristmas
tele_ _one	_ _orus
al_ _abet	Ni_ _olas
_ _otogra_ _y	_ _aracter
_ _antom	stoma_ _
_ _easant	a _ _ e

Step 45

Silent letters

Some letters are silent, but this is not as difficult as you may think, because there are some simple rules:

'k' and 'g' are silent before 'n'.
　For example: 'knight', 'knee', 'gnome'

'w' is silent before 'r' at the beginning of a word.
　(note also 'Norwich' and 'answer')
　For example: 'write', 'wrong', 'wring'

a silent 'b' or 'n' at the end of a word comes after an 'm'
　For example: 'numb', 'thumb', 'hymn'

Notice also the silent 'l' in words such as 'yolk', 'folk', 'palm', 'calm', 'half' and 'calf'.

Exercise 45.1
Write these words out two or three times:

Norwich	answer	yolk
folk	psalm	palm
calm	half	calf

Remember to read through a set of words from an earlier step at the beginning of each lesson.

Exercise 45.2

Read the words below and find the correct letter-group.

kn-	wr-	-mb	-mn
knife	wrong	climb	hymn
knight	wrist	comb	autumn
know	wreck	climbed	autumnal*
knew	wren	combed	column
knot	wrap	lamb	columnar*
knob	write	limb	solemn
knee	wring	dumb	solemnity*
knock		crumb	
knuckle		thumb	

* The 'n' is sounded in the longer word.

Try this

It was a cold autumn day and two boys were wrestling in the garden. One knocked his knee against a tree and became solemn. His friend wrapped the knee in a bandage, cutting it with a knife. Then they fed crumbs to the birds before going inside to write a letter.

Step 46

Silent 'h' and 'g'

The letters 'h' and 'g' are silent in some words.

silent h	silent g
hour	gnash
honest	gnat
honour	gnaw
ghost	gnome
heir	sign

Make sure that your pupil knows the meaning of these words. Some of them are likely to be new to him.

Remember to read through a set of words from an earlier step at the beginning of each lesson.

Step 47

-tion

suction

In a very few words, 'ti' says 'sh', which is very strange. In many, many words, 'on' says 'un'. If you put 'ti' before 'on', you have '-tion' which is a common ending and sounds like 'shun'. (The exception is 'question', sounded as 'questi...on'.) In these words, the stress is on the syllable before the '-tion'. There are hundreds of words like this. Many words end in 'ation', and in these words the 'a' is long and has the stress. 'Stress' means more emphasis on the syllable, spoken on a higher note than the other syllables.

Remember to read through a set of words from an earlier step at the beginning of each lesson.

Exercise 47.1

Can you spot the correct letter group that completes these words?

ti = 'sh'	on = 'un'	-tion = 'shun'	-ation
patient	won	suction	station
cautious	son	action	sensation
initial	done	mention	decoration
essential	front	attention	association
prudential	onion	invention	education
influential	London	inspection	separation
inertia	person	portion	ventilation
	month	addition	population
	ribbon		
	carton		

When the root word ends in '-it', the 'shun' sound is spelt '-ssion':

omit	omission
emit	emission
permit	permission
admit	admission

When the root word ends in '-ess' or '-uss', the '-ss' is kept in the ending:

impress	impression
process	procession
access	accession
success	succession
express	expression
depress	depression
confess	confession
concuss	concussion

In the '-sion' ending, the 's' sounds like 'z': 'television'.

Note that the only words where a 'shun' ending is spelt 'sh' are 'cushion' and 'fashion'.

Try this

Mary was a patient girl. She had to carry some confidential information to London. She needed permission from her parents to go but she refused to give her destination. They thought she had a strange expression on her face as she waited for the train. When the train arrived she waved goodbye and took her seat in the carriage.

Step 48

-ture

picture

Another common ending is '-ture', which we would expect to rhyme with 'endure', but it says 'cher', like a short sneeze.

For example:

capture   picture   lecture

Remember to read through a set of words from an earlier step at the beginning of each lesson.

Exercise 48.1
Add '–ture' to complete these words.

picture   mix_ _ _ _

fix_ _ _ _   pic_ _ _ _

punc _ _ _ _   furni_ _ _ _

scrip_ _ _ _   crea_ _ _ _

When the first syllable ends in a vowel, its vowel is long:

fu_ _ _ _

na_ _ _ _

crea_ _ _ _

Try this

Phillip took a photo and captured the elephant standing on a piece of furniture. He used the picture in a lecture on creatures and nature. The lecture was a great success so they asked him if he could do another one in the future.

Step 49

ie

pie
field

The letter-group 'ie' usually says the long 'i' sound, as in 'pie', 'tie' and 'cried'.
However it can also say 'ee', as in the following words:

field	thief	thieve	priest
yield	grief	grieve	piece
shield	relief	relieve	
	belief	believe	
	chief		

Remember to read through a set of words from an earlier step at the beginning of each lesson.

You may have learned the rule "'i' before 'e' except after 'c'", as in:

ceiling	receive	deceive
conceit	receipt	

There are, however, many exceptions to this rule, for example:

leisure	seize	neither
foreign		

The letter-group 'ei' sometimes says 'ay':

vein	veil	reign
eight	weight	weigh
neigh	sleigh	neighbour
reindeer		

Note also 'eir' in 'their'.

Step 50

be- re- de-

This is the big day: the final step in the course!
Many words begin with 'be-', 're-' or 'de-'. If you get used to this, you will sound out
'begin' correctly, and not be put off by sounding 'beg .... in'.

begin
refresh

decay

Remember to read through a set of words from an earlier step at the beginning of
each lesson.

Exercise 50.1

Add the correct letter-group to complete these words.

begin	refresh	decay
_ _hind	_ _mind	_ _lay
_ _come	_ _fuse	_ _fy
_ _cause	_ _gret	_ _fend
_ _long	_ _member	_ _sire
_ _have	_ _alise	_ _pend
_ _lieve	_ _sult	_ _clare

And finally

Now, how long did that take? Check the date you started. By now, reading will be safe. There are still rules to learn, but for most people this foundation is more than enough. Over 90 per cent of words are regularly spelt, and even the irregular words will have some letters that are regular, that 'work'.

If the new reader now has access to plenty of books, choosing them from the local library, large-print at first, and reading is made an activity enjoyed by all, you will have given your pupil a lifetime of pleasure and, I hope, enjoyed doing so.